THE GAZE OF LOVE

Ruth Patterson is a Presbyterian minister who has worked with Restoration Ministries, based in Lisburn, County Antrim, since its inception. Restoration Ministries is a non-denominational Christian organisation that seeks to promote healing and reconciliation in Ireland and further afield. It came into being in 1988, during the thirty-year conflict in Northern Ireland. Through a ministry of reconciliation, healing, hospitality and prayer it seeks to provide a place of safety where people can tell their story and be heard, where they can develop a vision, and where they can feel welcomed and loved. Other publications by Ruth Patterson include *Proclaiming the Promise* (2006) and *Looking Back to Tomorrow* (2009), both published by Veritas.

THE GAZE OF LOVE

RUTH PATTERSON

Ruth Patterson

26/5/16

VERITAS

Published 2016 by
Veritas Publications
7–8 Lower Abbey Street
Dublin 1, Ireland
publications@veritas.ie
www.veritas.ie

ISBN 978 1 84730 679 1
Copyright © Ruth Patterson, 2016

10 9 8 7 6 5 4 3 2 1

A catalogue record for this book is available from the British Library.

Cover design and typesetting by Barbara Croatto, Veritas
Printed in the Republic of Ireland by SPRINT-print Ltd, Dublin

Veritas books are printed on paper made from the wood pulp of managed forests. For every tree felled, at least one tree is planted, thereby renewing natural resources.

CONTENTS

ANSWERED BY THE GAZE OF LOVE

INTRODUCTION

What if infinite love has set its eyes on you for itself alone?

This was the question posed at a conference in New Mexico in April 2013 that I was privileged to be part of. It was organised by the Center for Action and Contemplation and entitled 'Intimacy: The Divine Ambush'. The main speakers were Fr Richard Rohr and Jim Finley. At one point Jim asked this question, and it has remained steadily and deeply within me ever since. I feel I would need more than a lifetime to reflect upon it and, even then, I would not have fully plumbed its depths. It was while living with this question that I began to be aware of what I can only describe as the gaze of love.

I have been struck by how often in scripture we read of God 'looking' or 'seeing'. As his inherent nature is love, I could equally have given this book the title *The Gaze of God*. They are really synonymous. A gaze signifies a seeing beyond a casual glance. It is somehow deeper and more profound. It carries with it a hint of intimacy and steadfastness, and a knowing that is enriched as much by the heart as by physical sight. It indicates something that is enduring, even eternal. It is paradoxically both unchanging and transformative at the same time.

Have you ever been in the presence of a beloved where you didn't need to utter a word? You knew each other without having to speak or do anything. The beloved was so awake and alive to the present and to you that they conveyed the message there was nowhere else they would rather be at that moment than right there with you. Such a person has learned the secret of being open, of letting go of their agenda or judgement or preconceptions (which can often be misconceptions), of making space in order to be present to someone or something outside themselves. They have moved in that moment from self-absorption to embracing the present with trust, hope and hospitality.

When you are the receiver of such a gift, you feel valued, listened to, respected, affirmed, comforted, and perhaps even challenged. Afterwards, what you remember is your complete awareness of the other; what remains in your memory is the way they looked at you with total presence. That is only a shadow of the unfathomable love God has for every person created in his image and likeness, and that includes us. We never move out from under that gaze of love. Most of the time we are not even aware of it, but that doesn't alter its reality. It's almost too much for our human hearts and minds to absorb. In the end, like all the other great truths of faith, it is a mystery.

Right at the very beginning, in the first verses of Genesis where the wisdom of the ancients uses poetic imagery to convey the loving purpose of the Creator behind all things, we read, 'The earth was empty, a formless mass cloaked in darkness. And the Spirit of God was hovering over its surface.' The loving gaze watched over chaos and darkness and, in infinite love, named – spoke – the life-giving word and set its eyes upon all created things and beings for itself alone. After each 'word' we read that God saw that it was good. The gaze of love encompassed all that had been made, and saw that it was excellent in every way. Throughout the aeons we, as humankind, have raped and plundered this good creation and have sought to clutch to ourselves what was always intended as gift: our task to be stewards. In pursuit of power and control, in seeking to put ourselves in the place of God, we have brought ourselves, not once but many times, to the brink of becoming a formless mass cloaked in darkness once again. Yet somehow the gaze of love always offers another chance, a new beginning.

As Jeremiah, the anguished prophet, wrote:

> I still dare to hope when I remember this: the unfailing love of the Lord never ends! By his mercies we have been kept from complete destruction. Great is his faithfulness; his mercies begin afresh each day. I say to myself, 'The Lord is my inheritance; therefore I will hope in him'.

In all his dealings with humankind throughout history, God is always the 'I Am', the eternally present one. Out of love, he allows himself to be so absorbed by us that he becomes fully present to us in the incarnation, in the coming of Jesus. This is the culmination of God's unfolding plan of redemption, for the restoration or bringing back of all creation into harmony, into an awareness of his gaze of love.

We all know individuals who are currently in a state of hopelessness. Buffeted by the traumas and trials of life; weighed down by burdens of anxiety and stress; imprisoned by feelings of inadequacy, regret, rejection or worthlessness; trapped in a pit of confusion fuelled by a sense of not belonging or non-identity, many feel themselves to be drowning in despair. On this planet we witness natural disasters on an apocalyptic scale: the relentless advance of a ruthless terrorism; economic crises; political instabilities and impasses; seemingly unending wars and rumours of wars; dangerous amorality taking root in some communities and a frightening legal fundamentalism in others. There is an increasing sense of alienation, confusion and aimlessness that causes many people to simply look out for number one – be that themselves, their family, or their own little group or ideology. These days, vast numbers, even within the Church – the people of God who are meant to be its image-bearers – are devoid of hope. They are disillusioned by the lack of prophetic leadership, by mourning, by a dearth of vision and by a cowering under accusations of hypocrisy, irrelevance and betrayal. This has been the case for many of the religious orders, with declining numbers, an ageing 'family', the bearing of a collective shame for the actions of a few, and a tendency to forget the courageous, envisioned, faith-filled walk of past generations.

As people of faith, could we begin to look on this seeming wilderness or desert (that is no doubt our current dwelling place), not as exile or a place of aimless wanderings, but as somewhere to which we have been sent by God? Just as Jesus, after his Baptism by the Spirit, was driven into the wilderness – a place where he forged his mission statement and then exploded into the world with the life-giving words: 'The time has come' – could it be that the gaze of love is wooing us in a similar wilderness so that we might rediscover our mission? Could our current dwelling place be where our purpose as the sent people of God (which is what mission really means – 'sent') is crucially defined and refined? Could it be that the 'days are lengthening', that spring and resurrection are in sight, that what we have viewed as something negative is the precursor to new life, and that this time, the only time we have been given, is really a season of outrageous hope? Outrageous in the sense that we can't control or engineer it, we can't conjure it up. The world will declare it to be foolish, offensive or crazy, yet its fulfilment could be beyond the wildest scope of our imagination.

This is what I choose to believe, what I dare to expect. It is the affirmation that, in Jesus' name, I fling against the darkness of these times. 'The best is yet to be' is not wishful thinking but a positive declaration of and belief in the loving purposes of God for individuals, for us as the Church, and for the world. How can we refuse to open ourselves up, even a tiny bit, to the wonder of such life-changing and freely offered love? Yet we do, again and again, and how we must wound the heart of God. It is God, Jesus, who is waiting for us to dare to open ourselves up to the love he wants to lavish upon us. He is looking at us/ for us behind the protective walls we have built up inside. He is peering through the windows of our souls. He is whispering his words of love and offering hope.

The message God brings is that the winter is past, the winter of dashed hopes, broken dreams and lost vision, the winter of fears, disillusionment, aimlessness and inability or refusal to forgive. New beginnings are within reach. It all hinges on awakening to the beloved within us. Yet still we hide; still we lock up our hearts, sometimes for good. We refuse to be seduced by the Great Lover. Maybe we do not want to grasp it because it is too risky, and yet having faith means taking a risk.

Perhaps nowhere in scripture is the gaze of love portrayed more intimately than in the Song of Songs. It is full of allusions to awakening, seeing, looking, gazing and pursuit. Yet this is not a commonly read book of the Bible. Maybe it comes too close to home. Maybe we find it embarrassing or it makes us uncomfortable. Did you ever wonder why? By and large we're not very used to tenderness, to gentleness, to touch – all of which are suggested by the gaze of love. A gaze can be tender, it can be gentle, it can caress without touch. We are wary of appearing vulnerable lest we be taken advantage of in some way. We find it hard to believe that we might be the one upon whom infinite love has set its eyes. As for God being the jealous lover (in the positive sense of brooking no rivals) referred to in the Song of Songs, it all seems a tad outlandish. Or is it? 'Love is as strong as death, and its jealousy is as enduring as the grave. Love flashes like fire, the brightest kind of flame. Many waters cannot quench love, neither can rivers drown it.'

Sometimes our experience of God is that of approach/avoidance. We yearn for more and yet fear it at the same time. When the fear or apprehension becomes too big, we flee. We turn away from what our real self knows would bring peace, fulfilment and release, namely the gaze of love. Though a whisper deep down tells us that we cannot escape, that there is nowhere God is not, we still try to flee. What strange, paradoxical beings we are! We try to hide, as Adam and Eve tried to hide in the garden. In so doing we deny ourselves the experience of walking with God in the 'cool of the day' – that time of intimacy and communion. We think we can make it on our own. We make it so difficult, yet it is so profoundly simple that, for us, it's too good to be true; there must be a trap. The length of time we take in our search for meaning, for full and eternal life, is commensurate with the length of time we resist the gaze of love.

Do you ever wish that you could relive the last number of years knowing what you know now? And yet we would not know what we know without the experiences we have had. We have learnt much more from the hard times, the challenging times, the times of apparent failure, than we have from the good times. When we are young we do not understand such mystery. We have to go through a certain amount of living – with its ordinary and extraordinary joy and sorrow, gain and loss – before we become more fully aware of that third dimension all around and within us. It is only when we have travelled a distance, leaving some of the old certainties behind, when we have risked letting go of some of our defences, when we trust that there must be something more, when we find ourselves in the desert and discover a hidden well, that we are perhaps in a better place to recognise (that is, know again) the gaze of love. The treasures of darkness are found by those who, however stumblingly, have believed that even when they had no visible proof there were riches stored in secret places, wells in the desert, light in the darkness, food for the journey.

In this book you will meet individuals from both the Old and New Testaments, people like Hagar, Ruth and Moses, and Martha, Zacchaeus and Thomas. These are people whose lives were transformed by the gaze of love. May they become as relevant for you as they are for me, and, as you journey with them, may you too be seized with the outrageous hope of transformation.

One meaning of the word 'passion' is to have an intense desire for something. How do we measure the intensity? Perhaps it has to do with how much we are prepared to give up or lay down in order to understand with the heart, in a place beyond formal knowing, that which calls forth our commitment, our desire and our love. Decluttering and shedding some of our internal baggage enables us to focus not only on the desired outcome of the journey, but also on the journey itself. This can be huge gift to us, if we are aware. Herein is the objective of this book, that each of us might awaken to our real passion.

In reading, listening and praying; through the beauty of the world around us; through the silence; through being present to ourselves, to one another and to God, we may risk enough to acknowledge our intense desire. As we do that I believe we will be surprised and awakened once more to the gaze of love and may know ourselves again, like Pope Francis, as 'a sinner on whom the Lord has turned his gaze'. Such acknowledgement can only lead to transformation. As we yield to the ever-present gaze of love, those who feel they know us through and through may be stopped in their tracks and ask the question posed so beautifully at the end of the Song of Songs: 'Who is this coming up from the desert leaning on her lover?'

AWAKENED
BY THE GAZE OF LOVE

CHAPTER ONE

I HAVE BEEN SEEN
(Genesis 16:1-16; 21:1-21)

The concept of a travelling people runs through the pages of the Old and New Testaments, creating the impression that the key protagonists did not stay in any one place for long. They were nomads rather than settlers. Those for whom desert or wilderness was home were used to moving on. Others living in the midst of more established communities often had to move – either as part of their vocation or because they were fleeing from danger – from place to place. This was also true for their interior pilgrimage of faith. Their understanding of God was stretched and challenged as God revealed more and more of himself, his nature and character to them. By the time we get to the letter to the Hebrews, especially in the great roll call of faith in Chapter 11, the vivid image of people of faith being foreigners and nomads, who touch the earth lightly because they have a destination in mind and a purpose in heart, is one that stirs and challenges. The one constant in the midst of continually changing circumstances throughout history was, and is, God's love. In fact, there is a sense in which the words 'love' and 'God' are interchangeable.

The pages of both Testaments vibrate with the passionate love of God for humankind. Most of the time, like us, the people of the Bible were not aware of living under the gaze of love. As a result they relied on the resources of a two-dimensional world to protect them, provide for them and lead them to a material utopia. Often when they felt the need to worship, the powerful among them fashioned their own gods in order to manipulate situations and people for their own ends. You might be thinking 'How primitive!' but we are no different. We do exactly the same, except, to our eyes, our 'gods' appear to us to be more sophisticated. When crisis and trauma hit, both ancient and modern are revealed for what they are – worthless and useless. In early times, many people, even those whom God had chosen and blessed, believed in territorial gods who ruled over certain geographical areas. This explains to some degree their great anguish, when in exile they cried, 'How can we sing the Lord's song in a strange land?' For them, the dwelling place of their God was first the Ark of the Covenant and later the Temple at Jerusalem. It was to take many centuries, culminating in the incarnation of the gaze of love in Jesus, to develop an understanding of God dwelling both among and within his people. Even today we still recognise, on the small island of Ireland, an allegiance to a territorial God. The question 'How far have we travelled?' in terms of our faith is still crucially relevant.

I always think of life and faith as a journey or pilgrimage. There is always more to discover, to be revealed; that is what makes Christianity such an adventure. If we feel we have arrived, that there is nothing more to discover, then perhaps we have not even started. Certainly someone or something very compelling challenged Abraham, who is described as our father in the faith. He heard an incredible call at a time when anyone else his age would have been enjoying retirement after a lifetime of labour. I like to think that under a night sky in Haran, twinkling with millions of stars, Abraham experienced the irresistible gaze of love upon him. At God's command to go to an unknown destination, accompanied by the promise that he would be the father of a great nation and that, through him, all the people of the world would be blessed, Abraham obeyed. He let go of many securities and went out, not knowing where he was going.

He and his wife Sarah were childless and in their seventies, but they had pilgrim hearts. Abraham has become known as our father in the faith because he trusted God to keep his promises, even when hope was gone and situations were desperate. It must have seemed that the fulfilment of these promises was long in coming, as year followed year without any sign of a child. At one point Sarah takes over from God and, following the custom of the times, offers her slave girl, Hagar, to Abraham in the hope that she will give birth to a son. However, when Hagar becomes pregnant, in her newfound identity and importance as the one who would give her master a child, she begins to make life difficult for Sarah. Sarah retaliates with such harsh treatment that Hagar runs away. Driven into the desert, alone and lost, with no identity and no name other than that of her slavery, Hagar's situation is impossible, seemingly devoid of hope.

The much-loved novella *The Little Prince*, by Antoine de Saint-Exupéry, tells the story of an air pilot forced to make an emergency landing in the desert, where he meets a little prince who has come from another planet. They form a friendship. The parable, for that is what it is, is the origin of many famous lines, which, for me, never lose their power. One of the most alluring is the statement from the little prince: 'What makes the desert beautiful is that somewhere it hides a well.'[1] Some of the most memorable encounters in scripture take place at wells. Wells are, and always have been, places of meeting. For Hagar, the desert becomes beautiful when an angel – a messenger of God – appears to her at a spring. The angel calls her by her name and assures her that God has seen her misery and has heard her cry. She is told to go back to her mistress, back to the place of slavery. It is there that she will give birth to a son, the first of innumerable descendants for this woman of no account in the eyes of her world. The name of her son will be Ishmael, meaning 'God hears'. However, it is the ending of this little scenario fills me with awe. 'Thereafter, Hagar referred to the Lord, who had spoken to her, as "the God who sees me", for she said, "I have seen the One who sees me!"' Later, the well where the angel appeared was named Beer-lahai-roi, which means 'well of the Living One who sees me'. The gaze of love gives Hagar an outrageous hope and empowerment, which enables her to return to the place of slavery, to the same tasks and surroundings. However she is changed. She has been seen and, for her, life can never be the same.

The sequel to this story, found in Genesis 21, is another reminder to us – if we need reminding – that God is faithful and keeps his promises. We never disappear from his loving gaze. 'Then the Lord did exactly what he had promised. Sarah became pregnant, and she gave a son called Isaac to Abraham in his old age. It all happened at the time God said it would.' But living in close community, as this desert encampment would have been, has its own strains and stresses, its jealousies and grudges, even among the best of people. At the big party to celebrate Isaac's weaning, Ishmael, son of Hagar and Abraham, makes fun of Isaac. Sarah is outraged and demands that Abraham get rid of both Hagar and her son. Abraham is upset but Sarah is a forceful woman! God tells Abraham to do as she says. 'Isaac is the son through whom your descendants will be counted. But I will make a nation of the descendants of Hagar's son because he is also your son.'

Consequently, Hagar and Ishmael are sent away. Once again Hagar is in despair. She walks out into the wilderness, wandering aimlessly, with nowhere to go. Soon their water supply is gone. She leaves Ishmael under the shade of a bush and sits a short distance away, unable to bear watching her son die. In her misery and despair, she cannot, understandably enough, hold on to the promise given some years before. However, once again an angel of God appears to her, calls her by name and says, 'Hagar, what's wrong? Do not be afraid! God has heard the boy's cries from the place where you laid him. Go to him and comfort him, for I will make a great nation from his descendants.' Hope returns to Hagar in this place of utter despair. God opens her eyes, and she sees a well of life-giving water for herself and for her son. We are then told that God remains with the boy as he grows up in the wilderness of Paran. Hagar's faith is strengthened. Her belief that God sees and hears all is affirmed. Her eyes are opened to the source of life. Once again she has been seen by the Living One who calls her forth to fulfil her true destiny as the unique and beloved child of God that she is.

The hunger in every human heart is to be seen, to be affirmed in our personhood, to have an identity that is recognised as being special, unique and beloved. For too many it is an impossible dream. For others it is an outrageous hope they fear may never be realised. The truth is that there are countless people who do not know that God is searching for them. How many people are there in our communities, especially in our churches, who are hiding themselves because they are afraid? They know that they are broken and naked and, instead of facing it, they hide their shame by self-justification or busyness. How much of the unabated tide of violence in our world is caused by the fact that, underneath, people feel themselves unloved, unworthy, of no account? How much of our labelling, hatred, sectarianism and racism is due to the fact that people don't feel that they belong and so will fight tooth and nail for an external identity, one that covers their nakedness, the shame of non-being? How much of our abuse of creation and of each other is because we have never truly known that God created us and calls us, uniquely and specifically, for a purpose? How frightening that increasingly, out of this sense of aimlessness or hopelessness or worthlessness, there are those who are taking their own lives and the lives of others because of their seemingly insoluble problems.

Steve Bell, Canadian singer, songwriter and storyteller, writes of the time when he was twelve years old and Jean Vanier (founder of L'Arche Communities) visited his home. He remembers the meal they all had together vividly, partly because there was not very much said but it was full of warm silences. He continues:

> Afterward my sisters and I went out to the backyard to play and leave the adults to their adultness. I was tossing a ball about when suddenly the hair went up on the back of my neck – there was a palpable shift in the atmosphere and ambience of the early evening bathed, as it was, in a setting sun. I spun around to see Jean Vanier on the back porch looking my way, enraptured by something wonderful. Instinctively I looked over my shoulder to see what it was he found was so delightful – but there was nothing there. Then it occurred to me that it was me he

was looking at. I turned my head back to meet his warm gaze and we remained motionless for what seemed like a long time. And in those few seconds I was born. I don't know how else to describe it. Somehow, his penetrating gaze flourished me in a way that I can remember today as if it just happened. We never spoke, something eventually distracted me and I went back to my play, but I've never been able to consider even the possibility of worthlessness since that time. *Because I've been seen.*[2]

Only when we are seen are we truly 'born'. Only then do we cease to see ourselves as worthless. As a result of all the wounds of the past, many choose to live in the shallows in a vain attempt to protect themselves from further hurt. For them, the depth holds too many terrors and uncertainties. However, if we can take the courageous step of opening up some of the shadowy areas of our lives to the healing love of God, there will come a time when we will know that we too have been 'seen' and life will never be the same again. There may be setbacks, times when we think we have allowed ourselves to be trapped or forced back into a negative situation. That is the time to hold on to the promises of God, to expect an angel, a messenger, who will remind us that God hears, God sees, and all will be well. Sometimes, like Hagar, I know that old wounds can be opened, but with the eyes of faith and with the angels of God sent, surprisingly, at just the right time to minister to me, I realise it is not the same and never will be. It is merely that sometimes old wounds can hurt more than new ones. And I realise, with deep and overwhelming gratitude, as year follows year, that hope has made me a prisoner. I have not resolved to become hopeful, rather I have been seized by it. It is the hope born within us by the gaze of love that turns the dream into reality. It will take more than a lifetime to be fully possessed by this, but for what I have so far, all I can say is 'Thanks be to God!'

The gaze of love is not a magic wand; it didn't make everything right for Hagar and it won't for us. One of the challenges in this ancient story is how to live in a community. The nomadic community headed up by Abraham and Sarah went through the strains and stresses of communal life, as do any family or religious order or group. They had their good points, graced with the huge gift of hospitality, and a prayer life that listened as well as talked to God. However, wherever human beings come together, we also find power struggles, jealousies, manipulations and cliques. Indeed, sometimes these things seem to be more rife in churches and religious communities than elsewhere. Abraham was a charismatic figure, held up to us as the icon of faith, but he had feet of clay like everyone else, certainly in the leadership of his community and the management of his household. Neither Sarah nor Hagar were without fault and were distinctly lacking in that generosity of spirit so essential to good relationships. This should give us hope. If Abraham and those around him, with all their frailties, were chosen to bless all of humankind, then so may we. Perhaps the key lies in awareness. As we accompany Abraham on his pilgrimage, he seems to becomes increasingly sensitive to the voice of God. He begins to know more of what plans are in the mind and heart of God for humankind. He is so conscious of the gaze of love that trust and surrender become the hallmarks of his personality. Like Hagar, he has seen the living one who sees him. As a consequence, his life is no longer his own. Community living still has its difficulties, but Abraham is now digging deeper into the well of faith.

Hagar was exiled to the desert, but it is there that she found a well. She not only found an oasis to quench her physical thirst, but also an inner well that would not vanish like a mirage. This was the well of faith, one that she could tap into, and from which she could draw encouragement and hope. It was this well that transformed the desert of her life into something beautiful.

There is a well hidden within each of us. Mostly we are not aware of it. Most of us have a hard time accepting the fact that we are beautiful. Perhaps both nature and nurture instil in us the idea that believing it smacks of pride and vanity. We're not talking about external beauty here – this is part of it, but not the important part. Jean Vanier says often, so often that it's almost like a mantra, 'To love someone is to reveal to them that they are beautiful.' This is true in human relationships, though they are fragile. Even the strongest relationships are not immune to interruption and conflict. But with God it is different. He is the One who created us; when he saw us he instantly fell in love and knew that we were good. It is his gaze of love that makes us aware of our beauty, and that beauty and revelation are always gift. There is no room for pride, but instead we must find ourselves straightening up in our spirits because we have come to trust the gaze. Often we may feel our inner beings are in exile, somewhat lost, despairing, unable to find our way and wondering what our life and our faith has been about. We feel parched in a desert. It is at just such a point that we need to pause and make a decision. Viktor Frankl, who survived a number of Nazi concentration camps, wrote in his memoir, *Man's Search for Meaning*, 'Between stimulus and response there is a space. In that space is our power to choose our response. In our response lies our growth and our freedom.'[3] Do I choose to continue along this road of despair or, like Hagar or Abraham, when all hope seems gone, do I fling my affirmation of faith against whatever darkness is consuming me and dare to trust the promises of God? The latter response leads to transformation, new growth and freedom. Each of us is beautiful because somewhere within us is a hidden well – living water – welling up to fullness of life.

NOTES

1. Antoine de Saint-Exupéry, *The Little Prince* (London: Piccolo, 1974), p. 75.
2. stevebell.com/2010/01/. Accessed 17 March 2016.
3. Viktor Frankl, *Man's Search for Meaning* (Boston: Beacon Press, 1959).

✄

CHAPTER TWO

TO SEE YOUR FACE
(Genesis 32:22–33:10)

Images of natural disasters, outbreaks of disease on a pandemic scale, the rapid advance of a militant and violent fundamentalism, anarchy and slaughter of innocents – all of these and more are vividly portrayed on our screens every day. We absorb these images both consciously and unconsciously. If we do not pause between such disturbing stimuli and our response, our reaction can be one of fear, anxiety, helplessness to demonisation of the 'other'. It is much easier to turn off a televised report than it is to turn off the turmoil they cause within us. We could conclude that no era has been as violent, disturbing and confusing as the present one. However, we only have to look to our history books to realise this is not the case. The psalmist alludes to such chaos repeatedly, most notably in Psalm 46. Descriptions of turbulent times, earthquakes, mountains crumbling and nations in uproar could be about the present day. But this is a psalm of total confidence that cannot be shaken: confidence in God. What ultimately cannot be destroyed is the place where God dwells. For people of faith, this is not so much a physical space, but an inner place where God dwells, a place that we have taken time to tend and nurture. It is a place from which the river of life flows, bringing joy to the heart of the One who created us, whose gaze of love is ever upon us, who has promised to be with us, who is always our 'I Am' God.

A refrain appears twice in this psalm, a strong statement that the psalmist uses to quell any doubts that the listeners/worshippers might have about God's abilities:

> *The Lord Almighty is here among us;*
> *the God of Jacob is our fortress.*

I used to wonder why the psalmist speaks, not only here but elsewhere, mostly of the God of Jacob. Why not the God of Abraham, who seemed to have far more faith than his grandson Jacob and who is referred to so often in scripture as our father in the faith? In fact, we are encouraged to emulate the faith of this mighty man. Why did he not even refer to him as the God of Isaac who probably lived a quieter, more obedient life than that of his wayward son Jacob? Yet here it is, unmistakably declared. It is the God of Jacob who is our refuge, our place of safety, our fortress, our defence. Then one day it struck me quite forcibly that the psalmist described God as the God of Jacob because he knew that this would give ordinary, struggling human beings like us hope. Somehow Jacob – with his obvious flaws, his earthiness and his less-than-spotless record – gives us encouragement. If Jacob made it through, and if, with all his stumbling, he has been held up by God as a guarantor of God's faithfulness, if God chose to be known as his God, then somehow, within his mercy and his grace, he could also be described as my God.

Jacob was a twin sharing his mother's womb with his brother Esau. Even before birth there was sibling rivalry. They were born fighting, and this was exacerbated in their early years by their parents – Isaac favoured one and Rebekah the other. Esau sells his birthright for temporary gain and, later,

Jacob (one meaning of his name is 'he deceives') steals Esau's blessing. Hatred for Jacob consumes Esau and he vows to kill him. Jacob is forced to flee and goes back to his mother's home place to work for his scheming uncle Laban. You might say like attracts like! On the way to Paddan-aram, as the sun is setting, he sets up camp near the village of Luz. That night he has a dream in which God promises, as he did to his grandfather Abraham, that through him all the descendants of the earth will be blessed. Furthermore, God promises that he will give Jacob the land for his possession. He assures Jacob of his constant presence and protection and that one day he will bring him safely back home. God is reminding him and assuring him of his ever-present gaze of love. On awakening, Jacob is filled with awe, 'Surely the Lord is in this place and I wasn't even aware of it.' He builds an altar there and names the place Bethel, meaning 'the house of God'. He then makes a vow – but it sounds more like one of his old bargaining tricks – that if God does all he promised in the dream, then he, Jacob, will worship him as God and give him a tenth of everything God gives him.

Where is our own Bethel? If we spend time nurturing our relationship with God – simply letting go and being still, consenting to his presence and action within – then wherever we find ourselves, not just in Bethel or in church, there can be a sense that it is a threshold place, a thin place where one's spirit is on tiptoe, where one is able to see more clearly, where we sense that at any moment the veil will be lifted and we will know ourselves in the nearer presence of God. It can be the house of God, the gateway to heaven. We all know places like that; we all have our special places. One such place for me is northwest Donegal; another is the island of Iona. Surrounded by such mystery and yet, almost paradoxically, acutely aware of the nearness of God, it's almost impossible to hold on to our emotional baggage – the animosity, the refusal to forgive, the suspicion, the desire for revenge, the self-righteousness, the bigotry, the anger, the fear – all those things that have forced us to flee from one another over the years, putting us into exile.

Fast forward twenty years of Jacob working for Laban, seven for his first wife Leah, seven for his second Rachel, and six for flocks and herds. He eventually becomes very prosperous, arousing the jealousy of Laban's own sons, and knows that it is time to leave Paddan-aram and return home. His biggest fear and apprehension surrounds his estranged brother, Esau. He assumes that Esau will still hate him for what he did and will seek to wound him further. He probably also feels some guilt for the way he acted and, in the depths of his being, shame – the deepest human emotion – for inflicting grief on his parents and much else besides. As he nears the borders of his own land, Jacob's anxiety grows. He sends messages of friendship and gifts ahead, in the hopes that these will placate Esau and prevent any bloodshed. He also prays. He sets up camp beside the River Jabbok and sends all his family and possessions across the river. He remains alone at night time. What follows is surely one of the most intriguing, mysterious and yet real encounters with God in the whole of the Old Testament. This is crunch time for Jacob; it is another conversion. Jacob wrestles all night with an unknown messenger. At Jabbok, Jacob finally comes face to face with himself. Throughout the night of his struggle, he finally knows himself as Jacob, the one who deceives. He faces his shadow self, his own broken and wounded past, his fears, his limitations, his bargaining spirit, his guilt, his part in the severance of relationship. He is not defeated, nor does he totally triumph. He refuses to let the mysterious stranger go until he receives a blessing. The heavenly messenger will not identify himself. In the biblical tradition, if you know a person's name then you have power over them. However, he gives Jacob, the one who deceives, a new name. The name given is Israel, one who struggles with God, and he blesses him as the sun is rising. Jacob names the place Peniel, meaning the face of God. He says, 'I have seen God face to face, yet my life has been spared.' He does not emerge whole from the struggle. He has been wounded on his hip. As he goes forward to cross his particular Rubicon and encounter his brother, he limps out to meet the new day.

In the distance, Jacob sees his one-time enemy approaching. Jacob goes out ahead of his caravan and Esau runs to meet him. In tears, they embrace. Jacob says to Esau, 'To see your face is for me like seeing the face of God.' Reconciliation, rediscovering the gift they are to one another, walking together again – it all happens in this moment after years of separation. Truly, in this encounter, God causes the war between Jacob and Esau to cease. He breaks the bow and snaps the spear in two; he burns the shields.

Certainly to see the face of God in the other, especially if they arouse emotions of mistrust and fear, will require a similar conversion in us, a seeing of things differently (which is one meaning of the word 'repentance'). It is something we need to face on our own, to wrestle with the demons that would keep us locked in our estrangement, to wrestle with the God who calls us forward to face a new day, to set aside all that would hinder us from meeting with former enemies because we have recognised that we are all sinned against and sinning, that we all form part of a common humanity. No matter how we have been hurt or sinned against, for the person of faith there will also come the day of reckoning. If we want to move forward, we will also need to face ourselves, not with what our personal Esau has done or left undone, but with what we have been responsible for and our reaction to Esau – what we have allowed ourselves to become. This struggle takes place in the darkness. At its deepest moment we do not know what the outcome will be. We can remain rooted in bitterness or we can see the face of God and live! Fear and courage, wrestling and endurance, despair and hope vie for the upper hand in this crisis of identity. As we hold on and win through to daybreak, the realisation dawns on us that we are not the same as we were. The struggle has wounded our pride and shattered any falsely based self-esteem; it has taught us a reverent and holy fear of the God who has made both Jacob and Esau in his own image, and presents us with the challenge of not only recognising his likeness in the estranged other, but also in ourselves. Jacob will not let go until he receives a blessing. As we dare not to settle for anything less, this is the blessing that we also receive. It is like a rebirth. With the blessing of knowing ourselves as beloved we can let go. We can surrender to the God who gives us a new name.

In the presence of mystery about to be revealed, this moment is not about attaining or learning anything else, but rather about letting go, about unlearning, about seizing the moment to lay some things down. This is one of the most significant challenges to Northern Ireland in our post-conflict era. It is with a degree of vulnerability, a newfound humility and a mind-blowing awareness of what is now being asked of us that we limp out to meet our new beginnings. For that is what we are doing in this present time. We are limping out, not in defeat but with a huge awareness of the journey we have made and a huge, if sometimes apprehensive, excitement for the next stage of the journey. We have survived the struggle. More than that, we are overwhelmed by what we have been given to see. In this life-and-death struggle for our true selves, we have seen the face of God – and are still alive.

It is that moment of total awareness that enables us to make the decision to meet a new day, to meet the strangeness of it – perhaps even the 'enemy' – and see the face of God in all of this. Because Jacob has seen the face of God, and has himself been seen by God, he can also 'see' Esau in his image. The gaze of love, recognised and authentically received, can now be shared and transmitted. There are several instances in the Bible where the moment of reunion between the estranged and the beloved family member is portrayed by running and embracing. One is that of the father running to meet the returning prodigal. Another is the meeting of these two brothers. Both tap into that which moves beyond even the mighty power of forgiveness to that of reconciliation. 'To see your face is for me like seeing the face of God.' John O'Donohue writes very movingly in his book *Anam Cara* about the face:

> The human face is the subtle yet visible autobiography of each person. Regardless of how concealed or hidden the inner story of your life is, you can never successfully hide from the world while you have a face. If we knew how to read the face of another, we would be able to decipher the mysteries of their life story. The face always reveals the soul; it is where the divinity of the inner life finds an echo and image. When you behold someone's face, you are gazing deeply into his or her life.[1]

What story did Jacob read in the face of Esau that day after so many years of separation and misunderstanding? When Esau beheld the face of his brother, was he able to gaze deeply into his life and sense something of the mystery of the transformation that the years and, in particular, his encounters with God had wrought?

And there's more! If we can risk enough, as people of faith, to take the challenge Jacob did, to choose to wrestle with the demons and to struggle with what God requires of us, there will be a price to pay. We may have to limp out to meet the new day that God desires for this island, or for any country in the world where people begin the process of dealing with the aftermath of conflict. The assurance is that there will be a future and a hope if our horizons have widened, if we are stretched enough not only to see ourselves as created in the image and likeness of God, but also those whom we formerly regarded, if not as enemies, at least with a measure of suspicion and mistrust. This is no sugary sentiment, nor is it wishful thinking. It is costly and it is urgent, and we may not get it fully right this side of death. It resonates with Paul's wonderful and mysterious words in his great hymn of love: 'For now we see through a glass, darkly; but then face to face; now I know in part; but then shall I know even as also I am known.' Jacob knew in part and acted upon it. He had many more struggles to face, but tucked away in Hebrews Chapter 11, written centuries later, there is a little verse: 'It was by faith that Jacob, when he was old and dying, blessed each of Joseph's sons and bowed in worship as he leaned upon his staff.' When he left home in the beginning, all Jacob owned was his staff. Throughout the years he amassed great wealth in terms of family, possessions and land. But the greatest treasure lay in his vibrant – albeit earthy – challenging and loving relationship with God, the God who had created him in his image and called him to recognise that same image in his so-called enemy and in all of humankind. So at the end of his days we find Jacob still a pilgrim, still journeying with his staff, still worshipping, still looking forward to that place beyond the end, where the sun rises eternally, where he knows even as he is known and where he sees God face to face.

The film *Of Gods and Men* tells the true story of seven Trappist monks murdered in Algeria in 1996, a time of military dictatorship and Islamic fundamentalism. Their small community was a powerful image of the trust, faith and love we've been reflecting on, a love that would eventually lead to their deaths. It was this love that challenged them and eventually forced them to make a decision about whether to remain in Algeria and face almost certain death, or whether to leave. Out of much soul searching and personal struggle, each of them reached the point of responding with the words '*je reste*' (I am staying). They stayed out of love for God and love for their Muslim sisters and brothers of Tibhirine and Algeria. A couple of years before his death, the Abbot of Tibhirine, Christian de Chergé, wrote his last testament as he reflected on the journey ahead. He called it 'When A-Dieu Takes on a Face'. In the last paragraph, he greets the unknown one who will kill him with these words:

> And also you, the friend of my final moment, who would not be aware of what you were doing. Yes, I also say this THANK YOU and this A-DIEU to you, in whom I see the face of God. And may we find each other, happy good thieves in Paradise, if it pleases God, the Father of us both. In sha 'Allah'.[2]

Christian de Chergé believed that in every human face there are glimpses of God, even in the worst of them. In this testament he spells *a-dieu* with a hyphen indicating a journeying towards God. The Algerian Church is very small and diminishing, but it has remained faithful in the most trying of circumstances. Central to its belief system is what it calls the sacrament of encounter, as it tries to understand how a tiny Christian community can manifest the love of Jesus in an overwhelmingly Muslim culture and environment. It is the call to enter into relationship with the other, a relationship that becomes a source of life for both parties.

In spite of both our ancient and recent tortured history in Ireland, there have been many inspiring sacraments of encounter, most of them among the quiet of the land. Through the grace and the mercy of God we have been enabled to see the face of God in one another, and especially in those who are very different from us. That is huge gift and it has not come without a struggle, as we have, often with a certain degree of resistance, allowed ourselves to be stretched and changed. Truly the Lord Almighty is here among us, and the God of Jacob is our fortress. However, there's always more. We're not there yet. Some of us may be nearing the threshold where we are leaning on our staffs and scanning the horizon for that ultimate new beginning. But our impending *a-dieu* carries with it the knowledge that the face of God is recognisable in our sisters and brothers. For others there's still quite a bit of travelling to do, as well as earthquakes, crumbling mountains, roaring oceans and nations in uproar to face. What will help us?

Psalm 46 declares that God 'causes wars to end throughout the earth. He breaks the bow and snaps the spear in two. He burns the shields with fire'. Year after year we see nations in uproar and kingdoms in chaos. Regimes that we thought would never be shaken have come tumbling down. We have been reminded again that no dictatorship can last forever, that arrogance will always, sooner or later, be toppled, that those who seek to rule by force, oppression and torture will one day stand alone, deserted. For those who honour God, there will be a new day, characterised by justice, mercy, truth and peace, a time when people will have learned the vital importance of integrity and humility. But there, beyond the communal, the national or the international, you and I stand, equally in need of disarmament.

We used to say in Northern Ireland, when the conflict was at its height, that what was needed was not a decommissioning of weapons, but a decommissioning of hearts and minds; in other words a change of attitudes. Peace would never fully come until that happened. We carry so much that we are reluctant to let go of. Sometimes we are not aware of the enormity of the loads we carry, not only from our immediate past but down through the centuries. We also know that in any conflict, no 'side' is blameless; together we bear responsibility for the long years of discord resulting in such anguish. One day I was looking through the Minor Prophets and I came across one – the prophet Obadiah – and I was startled by what I read. Often the most painful betrayals come from those who are closest to us. Obadiah really felt this way about the attack of the Edomites on the people of Israel, in particular upon Jerusalem after its fall to the Babylonians in 586 BC. The Edomites were descendants of Esau, Jacob's brother, so they were blood relations of the Israelites, descendants of Jacob. Of all people they should have been the ones to come to Israel's aid. Instead, they took part in their destruction and gloated over the ruin of Jerusalem. They thought that they were invincible.

Even though the reconciliation between Jacob and his brother Esau centuries before was genuine and sincere, perhaps it wasn't fully resolved. The brothers embraced, but what about all the stories, myths and grievances that Esau would have fed to his children and his grandchildren before that sacrament of encounter? And, no doubt, Jacob may have placed similar doubts and suspicions within the psyche of his own family too. What was the result of this? Centuries later we find the roots of bitterness, hatred and desire for revenge so great that brother kills brother and even rejoices in the mayhem. It's a salutary lesson that needs to be learned wherever there is conflict in the world. We are not only responsible for ourselves, we are also guardians of the future. What sort of message have we passed on in our families, churches, communities or tribes? Have they contributed to healing or to repeating the nightmare at some point in the future? We need to seriously examine ourselves and our attitudes. We need to do whatever is necessary to enter into a process of forgiveness, of healing, of a redeemed retelling of the story, so that God is honoured and so that when we are still, we are not hounded by the demons of bitterness, resentment, hurt and hatred. We should be carried by the liberating river of forgiveness, which brings joy to the heart of the God who will be honoured by every nation, the God whose gaze of love falls without partiality on both the Jacobs and the Esaus who inhabit our world.

NOTES

1. John O'Donohue, *Anam Cara* (London: Bantam Press, 1997), p. 63.
2. Christian de Chergé, Testament of Christian de Chergé, quoted in Martin McGee, *Dialogue of the Heart* (Dublin: Veritas Publications, 2015), p. 140.

UNDER THE GAZE OF LOVE

✻

CHAPTER THREE

THE RECIPROCAL GAZE
(Exodus 3)

There is an old saying: 'Someone or something may delay your destiny but they cannot kill it off.' If this was true of anyone, it was true of Moses. Born a child of Hebrew slaves, he was threatened with extermination, hidden by his mother in a basket of reeds, rescued from the Nile by Pharaoh's daughter, brought up a prince, took cover in the desert after slaying an Egyptian, worked as a shepherd in the wilderness, and, at the age of eighty, was commissioned by God to go back to Egypt to lead the people of Israel from slavery to the freedom of the Promised Land. What a life he led! The all-seeing, all-loving, all-knowing God – whose covenant with Abraham centuries earlier included the prophesising of four hundred years of slavery before the people would be led back to their own land – had placed his mark of destiny on Moses before he was even born. He was the one upon whom the gaze of love fell, for a purpose, just as it did upon Jeremiah who, when called to be a prophet in the turbulent years immediately prior to the exile, heard these words: 'I knew you before I formed you in your mother's womb. Before you were born I set you apart and anointed you as my spokesman to the world.'

Repeatedly in scripture we read of similar requests made to women and men who had become aware of the gaze of love and the calling that came with it. It's notable that, aware as they were, they all struggled with their response before their 'yes' or 'amen' – even Mary, the mother of Jesus. It is also important to observe that it is a gaze of love that invites reciprocity rather than a demanding hypnotic force. This can sound quite contradictory. If God invites a free response, then where does destiny come in? The biggest gift God gives us is the freedom to choose, even if it means not choosing him! And when every other freedom is stripped away we still have one left, namely the freedom to choose how we react to a situation. Love does not force itself, yet, paradoxically, in our surrender to it we are transformed. John Donne, the great metaphysical poet of the Renaissance, in the space between stimulus and response, knew such a struggle well. He knew what he wanted. He experienced the 'pull' of the gaze of love, yet at the same time his 'smaller self' rebelled against it. And so he prayed for God to batter his heart and for the force of love to overcome and enslave him.

> *Batter my heart, three-person'd God. For you*
> *as yet but knock, breathe, shine, and seek to mend;*
> *that I may rise and stand, o'erthrow me and bend*
> *your force to break, blow, burn, and make me new ...*

> *... Take me to you, imprison me, for I,*
> *except you enthral me, never shall be free,*
> *nor ever chaste, except you ravish me.*[1]

The surrender to love comes not through battering, but through awareness followed by a reciprocal gaze. Love is all about relationship; faith is about relationship and God is about relationship. In order for there to be relationship there has to be presence, a presence that vibrates in stillness and silence and so often seems to be characterised by absence. It is presence that conveys to us the message that we are fully alive. Do you remember at school when the teacher read out the roll you were expected to respond with 'Present'? That meant that you were there – at least in body! But there is another deeper meaning that is about being present in the now, in this moment. That's more difficult because we all carry with us memories, hopes, anxieties, fears and preoccupations of many kinds. It is so easy to cloud the current moment with our thoughts about yesterday and our apprehensions and wonderings about tomorrow that we miss out on the here and now. We all do it. It's human nature. However, it is possible to move to a place inside of us that is not quite so controlled and dominated by the relentless pressures of a racing mind and the thousand necessary tasks that are part of everyday living.

It is not so much about concentration or focused resolve as it is about contemplation – what David Benner calls being available for absorption, or being hospitable to the present moment.[2] What a wonderful concept! Has someone ever made a semblance of listening to you or greeting you, but you know their mind is elsewhere? There is a pretence of engagement but they are not present to you. This may be because they are carrying a burden or anxiety that has consumed them, but it can also be because they are looking past you to someone they consider more important, someone whose company is, to their mind, superior to yours. The message you receive is that they are not available to you even though they are physically in front of you. There is no hospitality to the now. They do not, either through their body language or persona, exude welcome. I'm sure all of us have not only experienced this, but have been guilty of it ourselves. Now consider something different. Suppose you are with someone whose gaze is totally focused on you, taking delight in you. The message conveyed to you is that you are unique, special, beloved. That is only a dim image in a mirror compared to the way God looks at us, is present to us, lets his gaze rest on us. Perhaps it takes more than a lifetime for us to fully and experientially appreciate that, but at least we can start practising presence, little by little.

Moses almost certainly had learned, at least to some degree, to be present to his surroundings after forty years' looking after his father-in-law's flocks in the wilderness. The day when his whole world was to be turned upside down, the beginning of a huge process of transformation in him, started out like any other. He could not have dreamed that he was on the cusp of a momentous encounter that would influence the course of history for thousands of years. Moses knew the flock and they knew him. In that sense he was a good shepherd. No experience is ever wasted within the economy of God. The years of tending sheep were good preparation for what was coming, namely forty years of leading a different, often wayward and unruly kind of flock through the wilderness to the Land of Promise. In the solitude of the wilderness Moses would have learned to be present to the rocks, the sand, the scrub, the flowers, the sky. He had all the time in the world to allow himself to be absorbed by this otherness of the world around him, of which he, paradoxically, was also a part.

So, perhaps, it is not surprising that on this occasion Moses was drawn into the presence of God by his awareness of his everyday surroundings. The fact that he noticed the bush was burning but not consumed meant that he was alert and totally in the now. Others might have seen the bush – a particular species that gives an appearance of flame and liveliness at the same time – but Moses 'saw' beyond because he was present. He experiences what Seamus Heaney calls 'big, soft buffetings', which 'catch the heart off guard and blow it open'.[3] He turns aside to see. His attention is caught and this is God's opportunity. He calls, 'Moses! Moses!' And Moses responds, 'Here I am'. In other words, he responds, 'Present'. The next emotion to seize him is one of awe. He becomes aware that he is standing on holy ground. He removes his sandals and then God identifies himself. 'I am the God of your ancestors – the God of Abraham, the God of Isaac, and the God of Jacob.' By this time Moses is terrified and hides his face because he is afraid to look upon God. There was an old belief that if anyone looked upon the face of God they would die. A remnant of the four-hundred-year-old faith tradition in Egypt that had motivated and inspired Abraham, Isaac and Jacob, this belief – whether superstition or acknowledgement – was growing fainter with the passing of time. It was one of a holy God who had made a covenant with their ancestor Abraham, a God who would brook no rivals.

Holiness, otherness and Presence established, there follows an amazing conversation between God and Moses. First, and very movingly, God lets Moses know that he has seen the misery of his people in Egypt; he has been aware of their suffering and oppression and has heard their cries. The gaze of love has embraced their anguish. All that has happened to them is held in the compassionate heart of God. And now the time has come for God to act on behalf of his people. We are shown in these couple of verses how God perfectly embodies contemplation and action, and thus becomes for us the sacred template for our own journey. 'I have seen, I have heard, I am aware, I have come, I am sending you.' This is where the hand of destiny falls upon Moses. His whole life has been leading to this point. The gaze of love had rested upon him even before he was born. For this purpose he was saved from the wrath of Pharaoh; trained in leadership and the ways of the world at the Egyptian court; humbled; and finely honed through flight and years of lowly occupation as a nomad in the wilderness, learning the ways of the desert so that it became as familiar to him as the back of his hand. You can imagine here a pause – and then God utters the fateful words: 'Now go, for I am sending you to Pharaoh. You will lead my people, the Israelites, out of Egypt.' Stunned by what he is hearing, Moses throws caution to the wind, resisting what is being asked of him. Referring back to Viktor Frankl's image, if the burning bush and subsequent conversation are the stimuli, any potential space between stimulus and response is swallowed up in Moses' protests: 'Who am I to do such a thing? You can't expect me to do it! Anyway, if I do go and say the God of your ancestors sent me, they won't believe me. I don't even know your name! And they'll never accept that you appeared to me.' Objections, questions and excuses are all met with an answer or promise, but Moses doesn't give in easily. He tries one last plea: 'I'm not a good speaker; I never have been; I'm clumsy with words. Oh please send somebody else.' Moses was certainly present, but he let his anxieties and fears cloud the moment, as we all do when faced with a challenging request. Even after forty years with space and time to reflect, he hadn't dealt with much of his personal baggage. In a strange way that gives me hope. God hasn't finished with any of us yet!

Whenever I have reflected on the internal and external clutter that colours our view of reality, I have thought of it as a restoration of hospitality between ourselves and God, between the various parts of our own inner being, between ourselves and others, and between ourselves and the whole created order.

I still believe this, but only recently am I coming to see the inextricable link between hospitality and presence. For Moses, this moment of encounter held many revelations, not least the restoring of hospitality to his inner self. This was what Rumi was hinting at when he wrote 'The Guest House'.

> *This being human is a guest house*
> *Every morning a new arrival.*
>
> *A joy, a depression, a meanness,*
> *some momentary awareness comes*
> *as an unexpected visitor.*
> *Welcome and entertain them all!*
> *Even if they're a crowd of sorrows,*
> *who violently sweep your house*
> *empty of its furniture, still*
> *treat each guest honourably.*
> *He may be clearing you out*
> *for some new delight.*
>
> *The dark thought, the shame, the malice,*
> *meet them at the door laughing*
> *and invite them in.*
> *Be grateful for whoever comes,*
> *because each has been sent*
> *as a guide from beyond.*[4]

In order to be present to anyone or anything, we need to be present to ourselves, not the self we would like to be or even think we are but simply to ourselves as we are now. Maybe we're a bit afraid of that because most of us have difficulty being hospitable to certain facets of our inner beings. So, instead, we do good works, we rush around so that there won't be space or time to let go and reach that still point where 'all' might be revealed. Some time ago I came across the short poem below, by Michael Leunig. It was accompanied by a little drawing of a person sitting on a fence looking up at the stars. And I thought 'That's it!'

> Come sit down beside me
> I said to myself,
> And although it didn't make sense,
> I held my own hand
> As a small sign of trust
> And together I sat on the fence.[5]

So it seems to me that learning to be present requires a decision (just like most of the other great healing tools, such as love and forgiveness) to be open, to create the necessary space where the invitation can be given, and to trust that as I sit with myself, holding my own inner hand, I am practising presence, not navel-gazing or negative self-absorption, rather I am in the process of restoring hospitality to myself. Such a state of being cannot be conjured up or summoned for certain occasions, but as I gradually seek to 'sit together' with myself, such presence will become part of who I am both on the inside and the outside – a way of being.

Is it possible to restore hospitality not just with ourselves but with the whole created order? Is it possible to be present to the non-human? Gazing at a sunset, studying a single flower or leaf, getting 'lost' in a beautiful piece of music, becoming fascinated by a bush that appears to be burning but not consumed – all of these things draw us out of ourselves into something that is other, but to which, paradoxically, we still belong. Our hearts are caught off guard by these 'big, soft buffetings' and are blown open a little bit more. Increasingly, through the practice of presence, we come to see that everything belongs. This was in the heart of God from the very beginning, when he looked on all that he had made, was present to it, and saw that it was very good. The wise old writers of Genesis expressed this great truth through the image of the Garden of Eden; its hospitality was open to all that was created and, because all were present to one another and to the Creator, there was harmony and rest.

What about being present to God? We wrestle with this quite a lot. We can only begin the process of taking it on board if we accept the fact that God is first and always present to us. Richard Rohr encapsulated this when he wrote: 'We cannot attain the presence of God because we are already totally in the presence of God.'[6] Much of our lives can be spent striving to attain the presence of God. We can also spend a lot of time telling God that we are present to and for him. It's easier than being open and vulnerable enough to simply accept the reality of his constant loving gaze. Maybe we try to earn it, or work harder for it, or long for some breakthrough where we'll truly know that God is here for all of us. What is needed, yet again, is a complete turnaround in our way of thinking and seeing. I love the image that we are always living in God's gaze of love. In all his dealings with humankind throughout history, God is always the 'I Am', the eternally present one. It is to Moses that he first reveals himself as 'I Am the One Who Always Is'. Then he adds, 'This will be my name forever; it has always been my name, and it will be used throughout all generations'. Out of love, God allows himself to be absorbed by us, so much so that he becomes fully present to us in the incarnation, in the coming of Jesus, who also describes himself as 'I Am'. This God is never absent from what he loves. This doesn't mean we don't face the challenges and consequences of our own deliberate breakages or rebellions, but it does mean that there is nowhere that God is not.

This is the message he was seeking to convey when Moses repeatedly objected to and resisted his request. God said: 'I will be with you. I promise to rescue you. I am watching over you. I will tell you what to say.' In spite of all the assurances, it was a frightened, inadequate, somewhat rebellious Moses who said 'Ok, I'll go', probably through gritted teeth, and who, in making such a reluctant choice, became part of what scripture calls 'remnants', those who make a difference in time and eternity. This is the paradox – part of the mystery. We are free to choose, but if we are seeking to be present to God, to ourselves, to others and to all of creation, it's not so much we who choose the way, but rather that 'way' chooses us. And, yet, still we might falter and stumble and prevaricate until we pause and allow ourselves to be absorbed by the gaze of love.

During forty years' wandering through the wilderness with a people who were slow to understand their spiritual journey, Moses' love for God matured, strengthened and led him deeper into mystery. He continued to struggle with his smaller self, as do we all. This was demonstrated most notably at Meribah where he struck the rock in anger. Perhaps he did not pause long enough between the stimulus and the response! In any case, God says: 'Because you did not trust me enough to demonstrate my holiness to the people of Israel, you will not lead them into the land I am giving them.' This may seem rather harsh, but it was probably necessary – it is never given to any one person to fulfil the whole plan of God. There is always the temptation to think we are more important or wise than we actually are. Humility cannot be bought – it is earned through experience, sometimes at a huge cost. The great leaders of today, and throughout history, are those who demonstrate humility. In fact, right at the end of Deuteronomy, where the death of Moses is recorded, the writer points out, 'There has never been another prophet like Moses whom the Lord knew face to face.' This is a thrilling sentence. Here we have the indication that, at some point on his inner and outer pilgrimage, Moses experienced a reciprocal gaze. And that communion with the 'I Am', that gaze of love, was what lived on after Moses' earthly remains were buried on Mount Nebo within sight of the Land of Promise.

When my father would sometimes get despondent or frustrated with the ageing process – this was accompanied with a sense of urgency about proclaiming the Good News which, like Jeremiah, he felt as a fire in his bones – my mother would say to him, 'Moses did his best work after he was eighty!' Whatever age we are, I don't think our destiny is ever killed off. The burning bush appeared at exactly the right time; with the gaze of love, God not only sees us, but the bigger picture too. This is the only time we have on this earth. We may think we've done enough, or we may be weary and disillusioned with 'looking after sheep', but it could conceivably be on this day, which starts out just like any other, that you or I might sense the power of the gaze of love that has never turned its eyes away from us. If we dare to pause between stimulus and response, metaphorically removing our sandals – as Moses did at the burning bush – we may hear our name and know the presence of 'I Am'. And if we dare even further and risk pausing

THE GAZE OF LOVE

a little longer, we too may hear the words, 'I have seen, I have heard, I am aware, I have come, I am sending you.' The hand of destiny may fall upon us, whether we are eighty or eighteen. What matters is that we are in communion with I Am, that we experience the reciprocal gaze of love and, being empowered by such a relationship, that we contribute to the vision of the Land of Promise within ourselves, in the Church, in Ireland, in the world.

NOTES

1. John Donne, 'Holy Sonnet 14', *The Oxford Library of English Poetry*, Volume One (London: Guild Publishing, 1990), p. 202.

2. David Benner, *Presence and Encounter* (Grand Rapids: Brazos Press, 2014), p. 24.

3. Seamus Heaney, 'Postscript', *The Spirit Level* (London: Faber and Faber Ltd, 1996).

4. Rumi, 'The Guest House', translated by Coleman Barks.

5. Michael Leunig, *Short Notes from the Long History of Happiness* (Melbourne: Viking Australia, 2011).

6. Richard Rohr, *Everything Belongs* (New York: The Crossroad Publishing Company, 2003), p. 29.

✥

CHAPTER FOUR

LOOKING TO THE MARGINS
(Ruth 1)

Halfway through 2015 I attended a celebration in Belfast to mark the anniversary of the official end of slavery in the United States. While we live today with the shocking knowledge that there are more people enslaved in the present than at any time during the infamous days of the slave trade, it is important to mark points in history where some of humankind sought, with varying degrees of success, to highlight the unalterable truth of a common humanity. It is important for various reasons, especially if, in so doing, we encourage governments and peoples to challenge oppression wherever it is found, and to actively oppose the modern-day slave traders. This celebration in Belfast was presented by the Discovery Gospel Choir, a multiracial Dublin-based group, made up of women and men, young and old, who both sang and spoke. In their presence and commitment, they themselves became the message, their one desire being to communicate the pathos and the urgency of what they believed so passionately. It began with one Irish girl stepping forward and singing the first few haunting lines from 'The Deer's Cry'. They truly embodied the following exhortation of Ronald Rolheiser:

> Forget about yourself and how others react to you! A bad singer on stage makes love to himself; a more mature singer makes love to his audience; a really mature singer

makes love to the song. Service is the same. Forget about yourself, your image, your need to prove yourself, and eventually forget about your audience too so that you and your song are not about yourself or about your people, but about God.[1]

As the singers made love to the song, we, the audience, were aware that at least half of the choir were from outside Ireland, those who had 'come in' with their hopes and dreams for welcome, inclusion, mutual respect, the dignity of work, and the opportunity to contribute to a better Ireland and a better world. Beyond even that, there was a palpable sense that, as they lived their message on stage, they were deeply aware of God – for them, alongside them, within them. The gaze of love upon them was so received and transmitted that we felt ourselves to be on holy ground.

The God of surprises looks to the margins, to inclusion, to drawing outsiders in, to paying special attention to diversity as the unique gift of his creation, which he sees always and ever as good. In his loving purpose for humankind throughout the ages, he has consistently looked to the outside for those who will play their part in its fulfilment. One such person was Ruth, the young Moabite woman upon whom the gaze of love fell. She was brought from the margins to become a vital part of the ongoing love story of God for his people. Most good stories begin with 'Once upon a time' and this one is no different. It initially concerns Elimelech and Naomi, who lived in Bethlehem in the region of Ephratha, which means 'fertile'. It happened that there was a severe famine in the country, so they decided to set out with their two sons and journey to Moab where there was enough to eat. Some time later they settled in Moab,

Elimelech died, leaving Naomi a widow. Her two sons married into the local culture, and life went on. Bethlehem must have seemed very far away, a dear but dim memory. It was better not to dwell on it, lest she be overwhelmed with homesickness and loss. Then tragedy struck again. Her two sons, Mahlon and Kilion, also died. To be without husband or sons or any means of family support in those times and in that culture (as in many places today) meant destitution. Then one day Naomi hears that the famine in Judah is over, so she makes the decision to go back home. Her two daughters-in-law, Orpah and Ruth, set out on the journey with her. The Bible says, 'They took the road that would lead them back to Judah.' If you like, they set out on pilgrimage.

On the way, however, Naomi urges Orpah and Ruth to return to their homeland. She is convinced that there would be no future for them in Judah. While being deeply appreciative of all they have done for her and her family she realises that now is decision and parting time. Hard as it seems, it is the only sensible thing to do. If they go back, Orpah and Ruth will probably find husbands from their own culture and be provided for, but Naomi has nothing but poverty and uncertainty to offer them. After many protestations and tears, Orpah turns back, but Ruth stays. There follows one of the greatest statements of love, commitment and fidelity in the whole of scripture:

> Don't ask me to leave you and turn back. Wherever you go, I will go. Wherever you live I will live. Your people will be my people and your God will be my God, too. Wherever you die, I will die and there will I be buried. May the Lord do so to me and more also if anything but death separates us.

Naomi eventually yields. Ruth's generosity of spirit and willingness to leave behind all that she has known out of love for the older woman warms Naomi's heart, making the journey more bearable. It is a nurturing of the tiny spark of hope that is in her – the only spark left after so much tragedy – that perhaps, when they reach their destination, their fortunes may somehow be reversed. Ruth's selfless decision has already begun the process. It is a long journey for the two women, but we read, 'They went on until they came to Bethlehem.' They arrive at the beginning of the barley harvest, causing a great stir. 'Is this really Naomi?' the women of Bethlehem ask. The name 'Naomi' actually means 'pleasant'. In light of this, Naomi's response is all the more poignant. She replies, 'Don't call me Naomi. Instead, call me Mara, for the Almighty has made life very bitter for me. I went away full, but the Lord has brought me home empty.' The name 'Mara' means 'bitter'.

The rest of the story makes captivating reading. Ruth goes to the fields to gather leftover grain and finds herself working in a field belonging to Boaz, a close relative of Elimelech. Naomi is roused from her grief, self-pity and depression and – admittedly counting on the integrity and wisdom of Boaz – uses all her skills and knowledge of her own culture to bring about a happy resolution. Ruth, from a different race, culture and religion marries Boaz, is welcomed fully into the community, and, indeed, is given a remarkable blessing by the leaders and people of Israel. Ruth and Boaz have a son, Obed, who is to be the grandfather of David, Israel's greatest king. Ruth, the foreigner, outside the promises of God according to the Israelites, chooses to go on pilgrimage, to let go of all that is familiar to her, to align herself with another 'kingdom' and, in so doing, is instrumental in preparing the way for the Saviour of the world to come. She is listed in the genealogy of Jesus who, in becoming human, was born of David's line. Interestingly, there are only five women listed in the genealogy of Jesus as recorded by Matthew – Tamar, Rahab, Ruth, Bathsheba and Mary – one a prostitute, one an adulteress and one a foreigner. It is hugely challenging, and can be very exciting, to see how God identifies with humankind and the manner in which he chooses to come.

What would have happened if Naomi and Ruth had never taken the road that led back to Judah, if they had never set out on pilgrimage, if they had never been companions on the journey? Would God's amazing plan, from before the creation of the world, have somehow been stymied? Ruth and Orpah are faced with the same choice – to go back to the security of what they have always known, or to risk stepping out into an uncertain future with little security. Orpah – good, faithful and sensible – opts for the safe choice, sticking to the well-trodden path of those who have gone before her. She knows the rules, the customs and the traditions. She will survive by being and doing what her world expects of her. There will be little excitement or challenge to her spirit. However, we must not dismiss or despise her, for, after all, isn't Orpah's choice that of the majority of those who lead moral lives, who do not do anybody any harm, who are pillars of society, who observe their religion? There'll be no transformation in her, nor will she be a source of disruption or discord. She will merely 'be' there. She stands that morning where two roads diverge and she makes her choice. In so doing, she disappears from the pages of history.

Beside her stands her sister-in-law, Ruth, faced with the same choice, acknowledging all the sensible reasons why she should give up the crazy idea of accompanying her mother-in-law into what, for her, will be alien territory. She gazes down the familiar road that would lead her back to where she could perhaps reclaim some of what she has lost and carve out the sort of life expected of a woman in her position. Then she turns in the opposite direction, towards the unknown country she has only heard about from her husband's family. In the words of Robert Frost, this road had 'perhaps the better claim because it was grassy and wanted wear'.[2] She seizes the moment, she makes the bold choice that will rewrite her story, that leaves the Orpahs of this world shaking their heads in bewilderment and confusion. Ruth leaves behind all that she has known – her country, her culture, her religion, her friends and her role in life. She gambles everything on relationship – the love she has for her mother-in-law – one that leads her into relationship with God and into being a key player in God's great rescue plan for the world.

In September 2012, I was sharing in a retreat with Jean Vanier, the founder of L'Arche, a worldwide movement for people with learning disabilities and those who share their life with them. At one point he referred to the three realities in life. The first he described as the reality of hatred, dominated by sadism and responsible for so much of the cruelty in the world. The second is what he called the tyranny of the normal, dominated by fear and characterised by the deafening silence of good people. And the third is the trickle of peacemaking, those who make a difference in the world. Jean Vanier then posed the question of what tips us over from the tyranny of the normal into that trickle, and he concluded that it is not so much something we choose to do as something that is done to us. We do have to be in some state of awareness in order for that tipping over to happen; in some way we have to cooperate. If it has happened to you, you will instantly recognise what I mean. Ruth was tipped over into a whole new life, a life that would profoundly affect the story of humankind forever. Orpah was seductively lured back to the tyranny of the normal, which can so easily happen.

God is certainly the God of surprises, choosing what society considers foolishness, going to the margins for his 'agents'. He chooses well! He knew the calibre of this young, unknown, destitute woman, from outside of all that would have been accepted in Judah. Ruth and Naomi succeeded because they believed that God had something else in store for them and, as we know, not just for them but for the whole of humankind. These two women had pilgrim hearts. They truly walked beyond what was the norm of their day, they risked together and, in all that they were living, still had a destination in mind and a purpose in heart. It was a long road back to Judah, probably filled with hardship, doubts and misgivings, but they did it together, companions on the journey, and they arrived at harvest time – a time of hope.

What would have happened if they had never chosen the road back? Within the timelessness of God, the God who is 'I Am', the ever-present One, this is a valid and challenging question for us today, the people of God. There is a sense in which Naomi epitomises 'Church' as we know it, certainly on this island. The Church, having once been in her prime, is now old, tired, disillusioned and, by and large, devoid of hope. People are no longer attracted to her. In today's world, with so many different interests vying for people's attention, the Church is often the butt of accusations of irrelevancy and hypocrisy, and, more recently, even betrayal. In terms of spirituality, vision and a prophetic voice, we have been in a time of famine for years, more than ever at this present moment. Having lived in a time of plenty, when – both materially and population-wise – we were full, now we are empty and our 'family' is no more. We are living the loss of so much – loss of numbers, yes, but also of vision, authenticity and reputation. Years ago we might have perceived our life as pleasant. Now it is full of bitterness, not only from the weight of all that has diminished us, but also from the half-acknowledged fact that we are partly to blame. Being unable to face our vulnerability, weakness and guilt, it is so easy to turn to self-pity, or project all the negativity outwards and even blame God. Why couldn't he step in and reverse our fortunes? Why doesn't he do something to give us, even just one more time, an outrageous hope?

God does not will hard times upon us. God is not the source or cause of our tragedy. He has gifted humankind with the freedom to choose, and so often the wrong choices are made – even, or sometimes especially, by the Church! When we experience great difficulties we have a choice as to how we react. In situations of desperation that seem devoid of hope, sometimes choosing how to react is the only freedom left to us. Do we take the familiar, honourable road to keep doing things the way they have always been done? Do we opt for the safe and familiar route that will keep us going our way but will eventually lead us right off the pages of history? Do we set out on a journey – not with excitement but because we believe there is no other option – so our hearts are heavy with self-pity, bitterness and despair that has nothing of joyful pilgrimage about it? Or do we choose to see what is happening to us right now as God's opportunity to begin again with us? Can we have the courage, faith, love and audacity to dare to believe that even out of this present darkness something redemptive can be born, a light can shine that will be the first stirrings of an unquenchable hope? It all hinges on relationship, the love relationship we have with God and the resulting love relationship with each other.

Somewhere within Naomi there was a memory of home. It was this memory that held her, especially in the years of grieving and exile; it eventually caused her to make the decision to take the road that would lead her back home. Joan Chittister writes of Naomi that 'she went back to become what else she was besides the wife of Elimelech, the mother of Mahlon and Kilion, "the leftover piece" – as the Hebrew word for widow calls it – of someone else's life. She went back to become herself again'.[3] How do we become ourselves again, or recognise for the first time who we really are – beloved daughters and sons of God, sisters and brothers to each other? Is there a memory of home within us? Are we aware that sometimes the homesickness we experience is our only guide? After all the years of grieving, exile and loss, both in community and in Church, what would cause us to set out once again as a pilgrim people, to take the road that would lead to new birth, to harvest, to a new sense of identity and belonging, to recognise our place again in the redemptive purposes of God? First, we could reject the notion that we are the leftover piece of a society that no longer sees the need for Church or a faith community. Yes, we are a remnant but that is not the same as a utensil that has no further use and has been cast aside. We can follow in the footsteps of the peacemakers, those who make a difference instead of, Orpah-like, going back to the security we've known, which has nothing of transformation about it and no threshold crossing to lift the heart with expectancy and excitement. Second, we could realise that we are not alone, that there are others who may be different from us but who are equally hungry for God and want to see his family restored, and who would journey with us if we let them. Ruth was from a completely alien culture, and yet God's purposes could not have been fulfilled without her.

For centuries we have fallen into the trap of seeing those who are not of our own tradition or denomination as somehow being on the margins or even outside the true people of God. By failing to look to the margins, what riches of diversity we miss! We have so much to share with one another as we make our way back home. God is calling his people from every denomination and none to commit themselves to one another with the same depth of love as Ruth showed to Naomi. He is asking us, for the sake of a world he loves and died to save, to pledge: 'Wherever you go, I will go. Wherever you live I will live. Your people will be my people and your God will be my God too.' That is the pledge we made to God, and to the people of God within our own faith community, when we started out on a journey that has led us through times of joy and grief, despair and hope, to where we are today – bent perhaps but not broken, battered but not defeated.

We are being called, challenged and stretched to choose the road that will lead us back to Judah, back to our roots, back to Jesus the Beloved. We are also being challenged to recognise our companions on the journey. We cannot get there alone. We desperately need each other, not only for our own survival but so that the world will see something different in us and will recognise us by our unity and our love. During traumatic times and their fragile aftermath, we may sometimes feel as if our name is Mara. Yet compared to so many anguished places on this earth, we have been and are indescribably blessed; in the hearts of many faithful people our name is still Naomi. We have a choice as to what name we give ourselves and people will respond to that. I believe with all my heart that out of these harsh times something powerfully redemptive will flow to the glory of God and there will be harvest and new beginnings.

I believe this not just for the churches in this country but for our sisters and brothers around the world. I believe it for all of us. God calls us to an even deeper union with him, within our own inner beings, so that each of us might be, in ourselves, image-bearers of his gaze of love. He is collectively calling us to unity, in all our wonderful diversity, so that the world might believe. We must travel together and keep moving forward in our calling until we come to Bethlehem. We are going back to our roots, but also to the fulfilment of harvest, back to where it all began, until we come to the House of Bread (the literal meaning of 'Bethlehem'), to where we begin again, and God begins again in us, until Jesus is born afresh in all of us today. This journey will always be tinged with sadness, for there will inevitably be those, like Orpah, who turn back to the old ways, unable to be grasped by vision. Let us not condemn them but rather release blessing upon them in our hearts. As individuals, and collectively as the people of God, daring to go on such a pilgrimage, we must have the courage to admit we do not know it all, that there is always more of Jesus to be born in us. This makes us people of outrageous hope.

We too are listed in the genealogy of Jesus and are a vital part of the story of God and his dealings with the world. There is gleaning to be done, there are journeys to make and risks to take. There is also the challenge to the wisdom of years to join with the vision and enthusiasm of the present day to become the place where Jesus can once again be given to the world – through women and men, old and young, black and white, gay and straight, lay and ordained, Protestant, Catholic and Orthodox – and beyond that, a dialogue with all those who seek to journey in faith according to the light they have been given. Despite all the evidence to the contrary, it is a good time to be alive. It is a time of glorious opportunity, of adventure and outrageous hope. It is the only time we have, but it is enough if we seize it. Ruth and Naomi went on until they came to the House of Bread, to the place of harvest and to their new beginning. Today, in this moment, we are being offered a new beginning as companions on the most important journey we will ever make. I am always humbled and inspired by the words of St Francis as he was dying: 'Let us begin again, for up to now we have done nothing!'

At the end of their remarkable and inspiring presentation that night in Belfast, a young African girl stepped forward and sang the same haunting lines that her Irish counterpart had sung at the beginning. I had this sense of all of our collective pasts, presents and futures being held together in an embrace of love in that moment. We were sisters and brothers, belonging to each other. The Discovery Gospel Choir then proceeded to the back of the church in silence. There they lit candles and filed forward again singing, 'We Shall Overcome'. In the years since it was first written and sung in that heroic struggle for civil rights in the United States, various groups in different nations have repeatedly used this song to the point of diluting its meaning, so for me, personally, something of its ability to move people in a powerful and positive way was lost. That night its power was reclaimed in a deeply inspirational, yet grounded way. We were all drawn from the outside in, into a place that did not belong to any one of us but to all of us together. There all of us experienced afresh the gaze of love.

NOTES

1. Ronald Rolheiser 'Some Guidelines for Service', from ronrolheiser.com/ some-guidelines-for-service/#.U7evjSe9KSN. Accessed 22 June 2008.

2. Robert Frost, 'The Road Not Taken', *Complete Poems of Robert Frost* (New York: Holt, Rinehart and Winston, 1949), p. 131.

3. Joan Chittister, *The Story of Ruth* (Grand Rapids: Eerdmans Publishing Company, 2000), p. 13.

❦

CHAPTER FIVE

NO HIDING PLACE
(1 Kings 19:1-21)

It is somewhat of a truism to say that we live in bewildering and frightening times. It would be so easy to become overwhelmed and to feel that we are living in an era devoid of hope, raising from deep within us many hidden, unacknowledged fears. It would be so easy to become desensitised to the anguish that we see in the media every day, to close our ears to the screams of millions whose only 'fault' is being in the wrong place at the wrong time, resulting in the loss of home, livelihood, country, and often life itself. It is too painful; it is too horrific.

In such times, many question the existence of God, or turn away from trusting in a God whom they hold responsible for such dark deeds. They have no awareness of a God who weeps, a God whose heart is aching and breaking, a God who is not some remote puppeteer but who, out of love, gives people the freedom to choose their response to him. They have never been awakened to the fact that faith – the spiritual journey – is all about experiencing relationship. This is the God whose loving gaze became incarnated in his Son so that we might know God. This is the God who yearns not for a blind obedience, but for an ever-deepening intimacy that stems from a recognition of Lover and Beloved.

As I reflect on the Passion, death and Resurrection of Jesus, one of the images that comes to mind is that of stillness. In the midst of all the noise and clamour of Holy Week, the only point of stillness is found in Jesus himself. On the Friday, it is his silence on the cross that speaks louder than words for all eternity. On Easter Day, in the radiance of a spring morning, the stillness vibrates with his aliveness. Nothing can ever be the same, as past, present and future are infused with outrageous hope. Central to Jesus' life was his communion with God. It is this abiding that gets him through the worst; it is indestructible. He dwells in the Father's presence. It is this abiding to which he also invites humankind; we are invited to dwell in him and he in us. We are invited – though the invitation may come as a mere whisper – to the place of abiding. Here we discover that still place in our day and, in the midst of all that is happening, we are found again by outrageous hope.

Elijah, who is regarded as one of Israel's greatest prophets, appears at a time of crisis in the country. His name means 'My God is Yahweh' or 'The Lord is God'. Like so many other biblical characters, his name denotes who he is and what he stands for. Many of the Israelites have turned away from God to false worship, giving allegiance to Baal, urged on by the corrupt King Ahab and his wife Jezebel. Elijah has several confrontations with the king, the best-known one being at Mount Carmel. There have been drought and famine in the country for three and a half years. The people are desperate. Elijah challenges the prophets of Baal, servants of Ahab and Jezebel, to a contest. Accompanied by amazing effects, including fire from heaven, Elijah – or should I say Elijah's God – wins the day and the prophets of Baal are defeated and destroyed, after which the rains come. This incurs the wrath of Jezebel who swears to kill Elijah within the ensuing twenty-four hours. Elijah, being human, is terrified and flees for his life into the desert. As evening comes, weary and dispirited, he sits down under a broom tree. It appears that he has succumbed to a deep depression, telling God that he has had enough and just wants to die. Such a reaction is hardly surprising after events that caused his nerves to be stretched to the limit, followed by anticlimax, then fearsome threats arising out of that most powerful of adversaries: jealousy. However God hasn't finished with Elijah yet. Twice he sends a messenger, an 'angel', with food and water as Elijah lies slumped under the broom tree. He is urged to get up and eat or else the journey will be too much for him. On the strength of this, Elijah travels forty days and forty nights through the desert to the holy mountain, Mount Sinai, and finds a cave in which to shelter for the night. Exhausted, fearful, full of self-pity, devoid of hope and curled up in the dark, he certainly doesn't expect what happens next. He's not allowed much rest, for God speaks to him and asks what must have appeared to Elijah to be a very stupid question: 'What are you doing here, Elijah?' If God knows everything, surely he knows that he, Elijah, has been zealously faithful but that the people have not? In fact they have openly rebelled against God, killed the prophets and now are trying to do away with him too. He feels like he is the only one left who has remained faithful – and look where it has got him! God doesn't say, 'I know. I've seen what has happened. Poor Elijah; it's terrible what you've had to bear!' Rather he tells him to go out of the cave and stand in the presence of God. Perhaps Elijah hopes that God is going to demonstrate his power again, in as dramatic a way as he had with the prophets of Baal, and make everything alright. What ensues is nature in its rawest form – a mighty windstorm, then an earthquake and then fire – a terrifying experience. However, God is not to be found in any of these – ways in which, perhaps, people expected to hear God. After all this drama, as Elijah waits, there is a barely perceptible sound, like a wisp of a breeze or a gentle whisper. And, in the silence, there's absolutely no mistaking that this is God.

In the stillness, Elijah becomes aware that he is being asked to let go of the huge achievement at Mount Carmel, of the fears that caused him to flee into the desert, of the self-pity and depression that consumed him, of the feeling that it all depended on him. He is being asked to let go of everything that puts up a barrier to simply resting in the gaze of love, a gaze that had never turned away from him. Elijah was not aware of this. He had become so consumed by his own situation, maybe his own importance, and certainly his own fear of persecution, that he was not alive to anything else. In the ensuing 'conversation', however, Elijah begins to see things differently. He is told to go back into the reality from which he has fled, to accomplish certain tasks, and is assured that, no matter how things may seem, there are still seven thousand people ('those who have not gone after other gods' [1 Kgs 19:18]) who have remained faithful. He is not on his own, as so often in the story of the people of God; after the testing, there is blessing. One of the things Elijah is commissioned to do is to anoint his successor. This is Elisha, and Elijah singles him out for his vocation by throwing his own cloak around Elisha's shoulders. So the mantle of Elijah falls upon Elisha, and the journey continues.

On the island of Ireland we have lived through tumultuous times, particularly in Northern Ireland. In 1998 we saw the gift of God and the triumph of reason in the peace agreement, followed in 2008 by a power-sharing executive. While many positive things have happened and many individuals and groups have courageously picked up the mantle of peacemaker and have been image-bearers of reconciliation, in the wake of momentous events and initial euphoria, there has also been a clearly identifiable communal depression or weariness. The pervading message from the largely silent majority has been: 'We've had enough. No more journeying for us. Let's settle down under our particular broom tree and hope that all these frustrations and obstacles will just go away.' There has also been what could be described as communal self-pity, where diverse groups feel they are the only ones who are being unfairly treated, intimidated and so forth. We feel that the British – and maybe to a lesser extent the Irish – governments and, indeed, everybody else owe us something. We have failed to see that the underlying answer to past, present and future difficulties is a spiritual rather than political one. We have refused the 'food' presented to us so that we might be nurtured and strengthened for the journey ahead. The sustenance offered to us has been the power of forgiveness; the recognition of a common humanity and the enrichment that comes from unity in diversity; the generosity of spirit that listens to others' stories and is accompanied by a restoration of respect; the ability to celebrate in a non-partisan way; and the healing power of gratitude for all that has been given, which produces a deep humility. Yet still the invitation comes, as it came to Elijah: 'Get up and eat or the journey will be too much for you.' There have been many 'angels' – messengers who have urged us to try even a morsel. For the most part, however, the offer is rejected. We are living in unreality. For me, the unreality is a two-dimensional living that has no real awareness of the third dimension, namely the Presence, the gaze of a God whose nature and essence is love, and who has been seeking to shape us and mould us into a people who have a message for the world. Whether from Northern Ireland, from the Republic of Ireland, from England or further afield, however well concealed or perilously near the surface, we all have tortured and wounded histories, both individually and collectively. If not addressed, they periodically erupt, usually causing anguish, further loss and misunderstanding. There has to be a different way, a way that may be only identifiable by a mere whisper.

This malaise is not only to be found in the secular world but also within the Church in all its branches. We claim to be people of faith who are on a journey where there is always more to discover about God and ourselves. By and large, however, our churches are little more than a mirror of our political ideologies, reinforcing particular confined attitudes that have little to do with the mind-expanding, heart-opening grace of a God who invites us to pilgrimage. We expect him to be found in the old ways of earthquake, wind and fire, and when he is not, we still go through the motions of our particular faith practices with little or no expectancy. Perhaps what we need to do is simply wait before him in the hope that he will find us in a totally new way. We are missing out on so much. We are weary, dispirited and fearful; we fail to acknowledge the issues that confront us. We have had enough. We look back to the glory days of the Church, to the times when we were riding the crest of a wave, where God was honoured, and maybe where leaders were honoured too much. Now even the good memories don't help, so interwoven are they with accusations of hypocrisy, betrayal, irrelevance, and so much else. Our prayer life is tired, vocation is called into question and the voice of the prophet is silent. These days I believe God is being relentless with the beloved of his heart, that is, with the Church. There is no longer any hiding place. We are being called out of our particular cave to stand before him, and the question is as stark as that to Elijah:

'Church of Jesus Christ, my Son, what are you doing here?' We can bemoan our fate, plead our stumbling faithfulness, wish, even pray that God would step in with visible, unmistakable power and sort everything out, but God is not generally to be found in such a way. He knows that it would be a nine days' wonder with nothing of lasting conversion about it. However, the gentle whisper of God spoken to the spirit of even one person attuned to listen, the awakening of one soul to the gaze of love, can change the course of a nation, of a Church, even of the world. It can be the birthplace of an outrageous hope.

The same could be said about how we view and react to the world in all its anguish, before which all else pales into insignificance. We can feel impotent, powerless and weary when we listen to the United Nations' reports of torture and killing in North Korea as being on the scale of the Holocaust; the raw suffering of millions within Syria and outside of it in refugee camps; the extreme precariousness in the Ukraine; the countless lives living under the threat of terrorism from Boko Haram in Northern Nigeria; the Taliban in Afghanistan and Pakistan; Islamic State not only in Iraq but spreading its tentacles with alarming speed into neighbouring regions; the brutal litany of rape and killing in Congo; sex trafficking; modern slavery; natural disasters; and on and on. We may be running away for our equivalent of forty days and forty nights because we are not seeing the bigger picture. Do we really desire to see things, ourselves and others differently? Have we had enough? Is there nothing we can do?

I believe there is something. It could be described as the next stage of our inner pilgrimage. It's something that we need to do as individuals before we can come together collectively in a new way. Nobody else can do it for us. It will involve us coming out of our particular cave to stand before God in a new way. We all have an interior cave, that place inside us where we can 'run' and hide if life gets too much. We may be cowering in fear, inadequacy, powerlessness, hurt or disappointment, but we present a different persona or mask to the outside world. Most of us do quite a good job of it. We mistakenly assume that the cave is also a place where we can hide from God. But this Great Lover never gives up on us. No matter what our life experience has been, if we are people of faith we are still pilgrims. So, eventually, we cannot ignore the call to venture out to that vulnerable place where we may hear the question: 'What are you doing here?' We may begin to pray the way we have always done, using words, sometimes endless words, telling God our version of what he knows already. This is not a criticism, it is one form of very authentic prayer. However, could we risk bypassing earthquake, wind and fire – in other words the expected, almost conditioned ways for God to communicate with us – and simply wait? With no words and no thoughts in what first seems like an empty silence, could we let go of our fears, our defences, our desire to be in control, even our dreams and aspirations, and simply consent to his presence and action within? Richard Rohr says:

> What's happening in [this] prayer is that you're presenting yourself for the ultimate gaze, the ultimate mirroring, the gaze of God ... You gradually allow yourself to be seen, to be known in every nook and cranny; nothing hidden, nothing denied, nothing disguised. And the wonderful thing is, after a while you feel so safe and you know you don't have to pretend anymore. You recognise your need for mercy, your own utter inadequacy and littleness, that

the best things you've ever done have been done for mixed and false motives. And the worst things you have ever done were done because you were unconscious [that is, *unaware* of my words]. 'Someone is giving their self to me! Someone is sustaining me,' you feel like shouting.[1]

I think this was Elijah's experience and it can be our experience too. It is after a time of waiting that we may sense something like a wisp of a breeze or a sound like a gentle whisper, and we will find that the fruits of such prayer are a new way of seeing our particular reality and that of our world.

Elijah was not the only prophet to enter into and to understand (that is, stand under) such mystery. Isaiah lived through the nightmare of civil war between Israel and Judah, and he foretold the exile of his people to Babylon after the fall of Jerusalem. Through him, God speaks words of consolation, challenge and exhortation. They could have been written for today's world as much as for the world of the eighth century BC. The people have been complaining that God does not see their troubles and that he is not responding to their pleas. After stirring messages of encouragement and comfort, he points out to them the limitations of their understanding, their lack of awareness of a God who is bigger and more powerful than all their imaginings and yet who, at the same time, knows and cares intimately, a God whose gaze of love holds, embraces and offers strength to the weak. He indicates that exhaustion, despondency and despair can hit anyone, even the young who are usually more resilient. Once again, the key lies in the waiting and the stillness. 'Those who wait on the Lord will find new strength. They will fly high on wings like eagles. They will run and not grow weary. They will walk and not faint.' As our trust in such divine encounter grows, God is given the 'freedom' to work within us, though, I believe, this is his own agenda and not ours. In an inexplicable way, something begins to happen in the unseen world, that third dimension that is all about us and within us. There are the faint rumblings of a seismic shift that creates the space for inclusion, for a welcoming of diversity, for the sense of a broken and beloved humanity belonging together. In a mysteriously 'understandable' way, we contribute to peace and harmony in the world and to the stirrings of outrageous hope. There is a dawning awareness of the unity of all creation, at the very centre of which is the beloved community of the Triune God, constantly loving, constantly giving, constantly present.

After Elijah's awakening to God in this way he is sent back to the very place from which he had fled in terror. Recognising his need for mercy, his own utter inadequacy and smallness, he goes back with a newfound confidence in the God who sustains him. He has been assured that he will find many unsung heroes there – those who have remained faithful. He knows now that God's work will continue under the earthly leadership of his successor Elisha, precisely because it is God's work and not that of any human being, however charismatic or holy. Perhaps that is also where our new beginning is. Wherever our particular pilgrimage has taken us, when God finds us his commission to us will likely be to go back to the situations from which we have come – or fled! There's an awesome responsibility resting upon us, those whom God is always choosing in this present moment, to not only look back, but to go back into the heart of the wilderness from which we have fled and there be image-bearers of Jesus. He wouldn't head away from the conflict, the despair, the anguish, but, rather he would walk right into the heart of it.

Whether we are currently aware of it or not, that is where God is challenging us to be as citizens of the upside-down Kingdom he came to bring. This is a kingdom where values often run counter to those of the world. For example, mercy holds sway over retribution or vengeance, the last become first, diversity is celebrated, and peacemakers are blessed. Almost paradoxically, that is where we will find ourselves seized by outrageous hope. Being totally present to the now is our route to a more fulfilling tomorrow. As we do so we become aware of the gaze of love that is infinite Presence. That is where memory is redeemed and hope is reborn. The mantle of Elijah, woven from the fabric of triumph and vulnerability, of glory and shame, of repentance and forgiveness, of memory and hope, will fall upon those whom God has already appointed to be tomorrow's Church. As we abandon ourselves to the gaze of love and to the will of God (perhaps these are the same?) for the world, for these islands and for our lives, we will gradually become aware of who these people are. We are in for a few surprises but, as we seek even at this late date to be faithful, we will find them walking beside us and maybe even hear them say, as Elisha said to Elijah, 'As surely as the Lord lives and you yourself live, I will never leave you.' Beyond their words we hear the gentle whisper: 'Be sure of this: I am with you always, even to the end of the age.' We go back with a greater clarity, not about specifics, but about God. We go back with a heightened awareness and renewed strength. We discover, as sheer gift (grace) that we are able to run and not be weary, to walk and not faint. For those of us who are older, any mantle that has been woven through our efforts and our passion, will fall upon – who knows? Be encouraged that there may not be one Elisha but many out there, as well as the 'seven thousand' who have not bowed their knee to any lesser god. As for the senior peacemakers and image-bearers, in whatever time is left to us our task is simply to keep on keeping on as pilgrims who are daily falling deeper in love with our 'I Am' God.

NOTE

1. Richard Rohr, *Daily Meditation, 21 February 2014, The True Self (Ultimate Mirroring)*, adapted from True Self/False Self (CD, Disc 2).

CHAPTER SIX

WHEN I AWAKE
(Psalm 139)

There is a famous line attributed to St Irenaeus, who lived in the second century AD: 'The glory of God is man fully alive.' Perhaps we are never fully alive or awake in this life. From mere observation it would seem that many people, certainly in the western world, live life on a two-dimensional level. In an increasingly secular and materialistic world there is little room for mystery. The third dimension, which cannot be physically seen, is unexplored territory to the majority. Many do not even know that there is territory to be explored or a journey to be undertaken. I say that not with judgement, but rather with sadness, as we in the Church must have failed them in some way if we have not, over centuries, managed to communicate the challenge, the excitement, the danger and the joy of a faith that is the substance of things hoped for, the evidence of things unseen. Perhaps I need to go further and admit that we ourselves are, by and large, strangers to such a journey. We talk about it readily enough, but walking the walk – the evidence of inner pilgrimage – is, at best, scant. There was a popular saying in the heady days of the charismatic movement that the devil works most effectively, especially in churches, by inoculating people with a small dose of Christianity to prevent them catching the real thing! The real thing is shrouded in mystery. Such mystery, however, is not characterised by confusion or a feeling of being lost, but rather it is permeated by a sense of wonder and the conviction that there is a 'knowing' that lies beyond our ordinary thought processes and the wanderings and imaginings of our conscious and often controlling mindsets. The huge learning curve comes from beginning to realise that this 'knowing' is not discovered by striving or doing more. It is about revelation or being given to 'see' something, which is the real meaning of revelation. It seems that in order to enter into a greater degree of seeing, of awareness, we need to unlearn or let go. This can be countercultural, for often the natural inclination is to hold on or to want more – more possessions, more reassurance, more security, more pleasure, more control. But in the upside-down Kingdom of God the norm is to loosen our grip on those things that we have clutched so tightly to ourselves, to risk trusting outside of ourselves, to choose to abandon ourselves to a different power – that of love.

I have some little grandnieces and they love the story of Sleeping Beauty. There is a routine that we do together, holding hands and going round and round in a circle, singing 'Once there was a princess, long, long ago'. It takes us through the story 'the princess fell asleep; she slept a hundred years; a handsome prince came riding … (at this point the eyes get bigger as the excitement mounts!)'. With the last verse there is almost an audible sigh of relief: 'He wakened up the princess, long, long ago', and of course they live happily ever after!

Children are far more open to mystery than us adults. They have no difficulty with the third dimension, be it entering into a story where the power of good always triumphs over evil, or being totally accepting of the God who loves us so much. In terms of our faith journey, it can seem as if we, and the Church, have been asleep for many years. Our senses have become dulled to wonder and mystery, our spirits chained to the earth, anaesthetised through distraction, fear, disappointment and the buffeting and brokenness that no one can escape in this life. Perhaps all of us are sleeping beauties!

This is at the very heart of the Christian faith – God's kiss of love in the person of his beloved Son coming to wake us up to the fact of our belovedness, to reveal to humankind that we are beautiful – broken, fragile, often misguided, but beautiful. The Bible is full of calls to awaken, to arise, to become alive. They give me such encouragement because I know that their source is always Love. For example, when Elisha the prophet was besieged in Dothan by a vast army of the King of Aram who was out to kill him, Elisha's servant was terrified. However, the prophet prayed, asking God to open his servant's eyes that he might see. When the servant looked again he saw, in the third dimension, the horses and chariots of fire of the living God. In a time of utter darkness and despair, God spoke to his people through the prophet Isaiah, calling them to arise, to let their light shine for all to see, for the glory of the Lord was shining on them. The Gospels are woven through with the call to awaken and to keep watch, most notably in Gethsemane where Jesus asks the disciples to keep watch and pray while he wrestles in anguish over what lies ahead for him. They fall asleep, worn out with fear, sorrow and confusion. The call to wakefulness is a theme that is reiterated in Romans where Paul says, 'Wake up for the coming of our salvation is nearer now than when we first believed. The night is almost gone: the day of salvation will soon be here.' The underlying melody of the Song of Songs – that love poem so beautiful, yet hard to take on board because of its intense intimacy – is the call to awaken, to become aware of the Lover who pursues us. Twice in this wonderful poem there is the exhortation not to awaken love until the time is right. For the princess in the fairy story, the time was right after a hundred years. Could it be that for us the time is right now, as we stand on the threshold of what seems like a world hell-bent on destruction? Could it be that, for those who are awakening, we are filled with an outrageous hope? Such hope is not to be confused with an optimism that vanishes when adversity appears, rather it takes root in the awakening heart that knows there is nowhere that God is not, a heart that believes that transformation is possible. Perhaps all that we have experienced to date has been in preparation for this moment, this now.

A useful, even essential, companion guide to such a journey is the Book of Psalms. These are wonderful, earthy, mysterious prayer poems and songs that emerged from the heart of a people who were awakening to the fact of who they really were, namely the beloved of God. Psalms were originally meant to be sung. At the beginning of most of these songs of praise or lament, of victory or defeat, of trust or despair, of the providence of God or the destructive power of one's enemies, you will find the words, 'For the choir director', often followed by a short explanation of where it is to be sung or its theme or to whom its composition is attributed, usually David, Israel's greatest king. Having been nurtured in faith through Irish Presbyterianism, before I was aware of the psalms in the Bible, I was aware of the metrical version that was passed on to us by our sister/ mother Church, the Church of Scotland. No service of worship was ever complete without the singing of at least one psalm. The language was a bit archaic and I didn't fully understand the words, but there was a sense that we were joining in with an early, almost unbroken tradition that stretched back, not just to the Reformation, but to ancient Judaism itself. The tradition

THE GAZE OF LOVE

vibrated with the reality of a God who was omnipresent, who held not only this earth and all that it contains, but the entire universe within his gaze of love. This was a God in whom one could trust, before whom nations would tremble and, at the same time, a God who understood the most intimate longing of the human heart. Throughout the ages, one psalm in particular, Psalm 139, has especially resonated with people as they too dared to embrace their true identity as the beloved daughters and sons of God. The psalmist, in a time of soul searching, comes to the deep conviction that there is nothing hidden from God and, after listing so many different scenarios, says very simply, 'When I awake you are still with me.'

This psalm initially can be quite awesome if we approach it with any degree of openness and allow the words to occupy a space within us that is beyond our rational minds. It is very intimate – some would say too intimate. Everything about us is known, every movement, every thought, every word, even before it is spoken. God is behind us and before us, all around us. He is Alpha and Omega, primary, immediate and ultimate Presence. In the first eighteen verses the psalmist tries to find the words to describe this total knowing, but in the end it defeats him. It is as if he tries several times and cannot quite get there. Each attempt leaves him lost in wonder. He finishes his first attempt with the words, 'You place your hand of blessing on my head.' An initial response might be, 'How could God, knowing absolutely everything about me, still want to place his hand of blessing upon me?' The second scenario indicates that there is no escape from the gaze of God – neither heaven nor hell, neither the ends of the earth nor total and utter darkness provide a hiding place. And so, helpless again to convey fully what he senses, he says, 'Darkness and light are the same to you.'

And there's more! It is not merely charting from the cradle to the grave which, in itself, might give us cause to wonder and even tremble. We are not only known from the day of our birth but from the point of conception. The story of our formation, from beginning to end to new beginning, the complex intricacies of what makes us who we are, may be hidden from all except the heart of God, from whom we came and to whom we will return. All of this is so overwhelming for the psalmist that, after saying all of these wonders are too precious and too innumerable for him to count or to grasp, he concludes with what may appear to be an anticlimax but what is actually very reassuring: 'When I awake you are still with me.' It's reassuring, yes, but also holds a huge challenge – to stay awake to Presence, and to dare to step across the threshold of the third dimension where we become aware of Presence all around us and within us. There are things we will discover only if we are awake. The poet Rumi writes:

> *The breezes at dawn have secrets to tell you*
> *Don't go back to sleep!*
> *You must ask for what you really want.*
> *Don't go back to sleep!*
> *People are going back and forth*
> *Across the doorsill where the two worlds touch,*
> *The door is round and open*
> *Don't go back to sleep.*

Often the temptation is to 'go back to sleep', but only in the initial stages of awakening. We are attracted to and, at the same time, fearful of the call to wakefulness. In her poem 'Advent for the Dancing God', Jennifer Woodruff indicates such ambivalence when she talks of God as being

one step too far away, one breath too near,
we fear lest he might never come again.[1]

We can spend much of our lives hiding from others and from ourselves, though, as we have seen, we cannot hide from God. While we hide, there is also a part of us that is longing to be found, yearning to trust that someone is searching for us. There are many reasons for this. One is a fear of exposure – yet God sees all and still loves us. Another is a fear of intimacy – I want a relationship but don't want to let anyone get too close to me. There's often a reluctance to let go – though the familiar may be uncomfortable, it has been my only security and where would I be without it? Perhaps I want God to stay at the edges so that I may have a foot in both camps just in case! This apprehension seems to stem from a lack of trust and a fear of surrender. Better to keep a little control. Control keeps us, at best, in the in-between stage of sleeping and wakefulness, with the stronger pull being towards the seemingly safer world of unreality, of a drugged consciousness. Better not to know that there is a 'doorsill where two worlds touch' than risk the openness and vulnerability that such an invitation to cross over might involve. Many of these reservations come, I believe, because of a lack of awareness that seems to stunt our growth and our heart's understanding of what faith, spirituality and life are all about. We can be so conditioned in our religious practices (though these can be very important) that they almost become God for us rather than God himself. We can give greater significance to the way we do things rather than to the relationship they are meant to nurture. We are left with the container of our particular belief system rather than the content, which is, or should be, an ever-deepening intimacy with the Beloved from which many fruits may flow. If our relationship is properly nurtured, the fruits will be beyond imagination. Our prime motivation, however, is to seek to be present in the eternal now to the Beloved, beyond our controlling thoughts and manipulating minds, and to know, in a place beyond formal knowing, that there is a reciprocal desire. God wants intimacy with us more than we want it with him. Even in prayer we feel we must strive for perfection; we wonder if we are doing it right and how we are measuring up. It goes against the grain to let all that go and to discover, or be found again by being, by Presence, by now, by this moment, by the I Am.

Who am I? Who are you? Or who do you think you are? These are not the same questions. Who I am and who I think I am may be two very different things. When I think of myself, I know people often only see the public persona, someone who seems confident enough, faithful enough, joyful enough, loving enough, peaceful enough. However, behind all that there is also the other – the one who is vulnerable, fearful, insecure, longing for acceptance, questioning and, at times, despairing. Who is the real me – this or the other? Both are true. And both are held within the gaze of love.

It is everyone's journey, isn't it? We come from God and we are returning to God. Somewhere along the way, because of life experience, we get cracked or broken, losing our way, but, in the mystery of the grace and mercy of God, it is that very cracking that becomes our salvation, our way to discovering again what we once 'knew' but have 'forgotten'. In my schooldays, we had to wade our way through Wordsworth's interminable ode 'Intimations of Immortality from Recollections of Early Childhood'. While being bored with much of it as a young person, like so much else, part of it now comes back to me with an unmistakable ring of truth.

Not in entire forgetfulness
and not in utter nakedness,
but trailing clouds of glory do we come
from God who is our home;

And later Wordsworth concludes:

At length the man perceives it pass away
And fade into the light of common day.[2]

I would say that most of us have no problem acknowledging, at least privately, that we are poor, small and broken, and that a large percentage of our lives is spent dealing with excess baggage. The wounds, both real and imagined, inflicted by life, by circumstances, by others, by impersonal institutions, by our own actions and reactions, can go so deep that we may think the only way to cope is to box them away in an inner vault, throw away the key and then construct those 'necessary' barricades to protect ourselves against further wounding. We then add to that a shot of anaesthetic to deaden not only our pain but also our sensitivity to the melody of mercy, hope and love that keeps knocking on the door of our inner selves. All of this represents a large percentage of humankind, certainly in the western world, who outwardly present a coping, even successful persona, but are inwardly inhibited, stressed, controlling and often in anguish. The word anguish comes from the Latin *angustus*, which means narrow or constricted. Anguish is the pain of a soul confined and restricted. It can be impossible for humans to think outside of time and space. We are in anguish as we seek to feel our way into the mystery of God. He is not confined by these things and yet, at the same time, in a place beyond knowing, we catch glimpses of this eternal now of God, he who is always the 'I Am'. Whenever we catch that glimpse, it increases our aching and yearning, our anguish to be at home with this God who, having taken on our humanity, becomes constricted and confined for our sakes, and weeps from a broken heart over those who still cannot hear or understand something of the mystery of such love.

Touch, tenderness, gentleness, compassion and love are all the language of intimacy. Why do we find them so difficult? We feel safer remaining 'in our heads'. Those who have suffered often move more readily from the head to the heart, beyond words, to where presence and touch are more important. They have a receptivity to this silent language that some of those who remain locked in their heads have no understanding of. We have to be loved before we can love, before the walls come down, before we can see clearly. By building interior walls to self-protect, we find ourselves in inner darkness. The light can't get in. How can we wake up? Who has the power to break the spell that has held us captive and caused us to live in the land of shadows? We must put ourselves in a place of preparedness. One of the ways to do this is to begin internally decluttering, letting go of grudges or burdens we persist in carrying, and choosing to take a little space where we can wind down, switch off, and affirm that we are in the presence of the God who loves us and yearns to reveal to us that we are beautiful. Sooner or later the kiss will come and we will wake up a little more, and this will continue for as long as our earthly journey does. The secret lies in being willing to climb down, to go on that inner journey, to realise that, yes, in the secret place where the fears and anxieties lurk there is also a hidden place of intimacy where there can be a meeting of Lover and beloved. And that is a form of prayer.

The psalmist knew this. In the latter part of the psalm, he pleads with God to deliver him from his enemies. The language is unambiguous and strong. Perhaps he realises that his biggest enemies are those within himself. Certainly Nan Merrill, in her wonderful book *Psalms for Praying*, indicates this when she paraphrases the psalmist's words, thus:

> O that you would vanquish my fears, Beloved;
> O that ignorance and suffering would depart from me –
> My ego separates me from true abandonment
> to surrendering myself into your hands!
> Yet are these not the very thorns that focus my thoughts
> upon you?[3]

In her preface Merrill says, 'Praying the psalms with heartfelt attention and intention can be a step toward our souls awakening to the Love Consciousness being brought into the light out of the ashes of terror and destruction in our day.'[4] This experience and knowledge is absolutely vital for modern living. As people of faith we cannot ignore the harsh reality of this world, a reality that is lived by the majority of the world's population. It is into such a world that God comes, not to a palace but to a manger, with threats on his life, becoming a fugitive and a refugee. We awaken to the fact of our belovedness, and, if the experience is real, we also become aware of a passionate God who will not rest until everything once again belongs, is awakened and redeemed. I remember someone once saying, 'God is not our uncle. God is an earthquake!' This is the compelling and challenging side of believing to which we are also called to awaken. We can only do so out of the security of knowing we are loved. In that awareness we can pray for God to search us and know our hearts, to test us and know our thoughts, to point out anything within that offends, and to lead us along the path of life in all its fullness.

Let Jennifer Woodruff once again put her words and her 'Amen' on such a prayer.

O in the darkness of a night gone out
come find me once again, descend, be born,
be racked by wind and crucified and torn
yet never stop the dance. How could I doubt
your peace more frightening than any pain
your dark embrace that burns and purifies,
the searching sharp enchantment of your eyes,
the absolute perfection of your flame?[5]

NOTES

1. Jennifer L. Woodruff, 'Advent for the Dancing God' from *Weaving* (Nashville: The Upper Room, 2001).

2. William Wordsworth, 'Ode', *The Norton Anthology of English Literature*, Fifth Edition, Vol. 2, M. H. Abrams, general ed. (London: W.W. Norton & Co, Ltd., 1986), p. 211.

3. Nan Merrill, *Psalms for Praying* (New York: Continuum, 2011), p. 279.

4. Ibid., p. vii.

5. Jennifer L. Woodruff, 'Advent for the Dancing God'.

CALLED BY
THE GAZE OF LOVE

❦

CHAPTER SEVEN

THE GAZE THAT INVITES
(John 1:35-51)

We now move from the Old Testament to the New Testament. Although chronologically there is a gap of about four hundred years, there is no gap whatsoever in terms of God's faithfulness and gaze of love. However, with the New Testament the gaze of love is incarnated – made manifest – in Jesus. We enter the uninterrupted flow just as Jesus is about to begin his public ministry as recorded for us in John's Gospel.

'Come and see' are deceptively simple words. They are found several times in the very first chapter of John's Gospel and are the essence of what the journey of faith is all about: action (come) and contemplation (see). Both these components are vital for life as companions of Jesus. Most of us feel more comfortable with the action side of things. This is very important, but unless we are also taking time to 'see', then the action can sometimes be misplaced or ineffective. We are rather scared of being still, of taking the time to see. We strive to be accepted – by other people, but maybe especially, if unconsciously, by God. It's as though something within us militates against accepting that we are loved just as we are. It seems too good to be true, so we do what we think is the next best thing, we busy ourselves doing things to try to please God. Our life experiences – especially if they have involved control, manipulation, rejections, abandonments and fear – can colour and distort not only our human relationships, but the image we have of God. Is it any wonder, then, that people who may have a longing for a deeper connection with God fail to take time to see, in case their fears are realised that they are inherently unlovable, that they have been judged and found wanting, that vibrant faith and spiritual pilgrimage are for everyone else but not for them? We are all a bit like that; it is hard to come to grips with the realisation that we are being asked to completely readjust our thinking, that it is not about more but about less, about letting go in order that we might rediscover, or rather be found again by the One who loves us unconditionally and forever. How do we begin to let go enough to trust, even a little, that each of us is embraced by such a gaze of love? We can wonder about it, question it, doubt it and yearn for it, but the only way to know it is to come and see.

John the Baptist was the great forerunner, the one who prepared the way for the coming of Jesus. People were flocking to hear him and to be baptised. Some were so attracted by who he was, by his integrity, authenticity and the message he proclaimed that they became his disciples. Prior to Jesus' Baptism, John may have thought he knew all there was to know about his cousin, but when he saw the Spirit descending his eyes were opened and he knew that this was the One: 'There is the Lamb of God.' It was the fulfilment of his life's work. The moment had come and his heart was resounding with a tumultuous 'Yes'. At the same time he was human, so the lurking shadow side must have been an aching loneliness. John must have known that this was the end of his mission. The spotlight was then turned on Jesus. John's last act of love, carried out with a generous heart, is to let go of all that he had been, his task now complete. Love and suffering meet in John the Baptist as he declares fully and unequivocally who

Jesus is, before stepping back. This is confirmed for him when, almost immediately, two of his closest companions turn away and follow Jesus. They leave the old dispensation behind and set out on a journey that will mould them and last for the rest of their lives. They do not know where this new way will lead them, they only know that they have to follow. All that will ensue will not be a rejection of their tradition, nor of what they had experienced with John, but rather an opening out, a fulfilment of all that has gone before.

We can picture them, perhaps having impulsively turned to go after Jesus and then feeling a little nervous, walking a distance behind him. Jesus knows they are there. He sees more than they realise. He sees the seeking in them, the questioning, the desire. Then he asks the seemingly simple, yet deeply searching question, 'What do you want?' Taken unawares, they do not know how to respond, so they answer with another seemingly innocuous question, 'Rabbi, where are you staying?' Jesus knows that the real question is, 'Who are you? Where or from whom have you come? What is it about you that we feel compelled to find out more about?' They perhaps thought they knew all there was to know about believing in God, but now something has shifted and they realise that they have scarcely even begun. Then Jesus issues the invitation, 'Come and see'. So they go and stay (abide) the rest of the day. Jesus frequently uses the word 'abide' most notably in John, Chapter 15, where he issues the invitation to a mutual abiding. To abide means to stay in a particular place, but it is also used to indicate a close friendship, a communion, where we dwell in one another. The real home of Jesus is the Father. He dwells in the Father's presence. It is this awareness that he invites humankind into also – that we dwell in him and he in us.

I find these few verses immensely exciting, challenging and poignant. They are about journey, about letting go and new beginnings, about a dawning awareness, about invitation and response, about not knowing and risking. One word that would sum all of that up is faith. Faith is steadfast but, paradoxically, always changing, expanding, daring and leading us deeper into mystery. We can become so used to our specific faith practice, especially if we have been brought up in a particular religious denomination, that the way we have always done things becomes an integral part of who we are. That, of course, is important. The tradition that has nurtured us in the faith has given us so much to be grateful for. But does it stop there? Do we think this is it? That there's really not much more to know? Have we become settlers rather than pilgrims? In that sense, have we made a god out of our denomination or our local church, seeing it as the end rather than the means of leading people into a deeper understanding of what it means to be a follower or companion of Jesus? It is not easy to step out from the familiar, to say goodbye to some of what we thought were certainties, to unlearn what we once held to be infallible. Sometimes we risk misunderstanding and even outright rejection because, in stepping out, we have challenged the status quo.

We may have reached a plateau or resting place in our faith some time ago. Then, one day, we may hear something or have an encounter or experience and everything changes. We discover an urge to find out more. Just as Jesus, long ago, looked and saw them following, so he looks and sees us. The look that Jesus directs towards us sees deeply into who we are, and he asks us, 'What do you want?' What do we really want, when all lesser wants are stripped away? We may answer with another question, perhaps trying to deflect the loving attention away from us. 'Where are you staying?' This is another deceptively simple question with profound connotations. Where is Jesus staying today? Where do we find him? We might discover him in some surprising places, yet be unable to locate him in some of the more conventional and expected places. Today, we may find him more readily on the margins, among the weak and the vulnerable. Could he also be dwelling within us? The awesome truth is that he is, but our awareness levels are so dulled that we cannot discern it. Sometimes it feels that most of us in our parishes and congregations are in a similar drugged state. Think what could happen on the island of Ireland if all those who professed to be followers of Jesus awakened to mutual abiding. If we take a moment to be still amidst all of this wondering, questioning and seeking, and we pause under the gaze of love, we too may hear the invitation: 'Come and see.' In the coming and in the seeing, we will be led a little deeper into the mystery of infinite, unfathomable love, the love of God made visible to us in Jesus. We may understand more clearly what we need to let go of in order to focus on what is most important. We will then follow him, on both the inner and the outer journey, to the place of his abiding.

In these few verses in John's Gospel, we have action and contemplation personified. Andrew is so excited by spending several hours with Jesus that he can hardly wait to tell his brother Simon. The first thing he does is find Simon and the news bursts out of him, 'We have found the Messiah'. Simon's response is not recorded for us here. Andrew, however, must have been persuasive, or aroused Simon's curiosity, because the result was a hugely significant encounter. Once again it's the gaze of love that rests upon Simon. Jesus looks intently at him. In other words, Jesus sees what no one else can see. He sees who he is and who he is becoming. 'You are Simon, the son of John but you will be called Cephas (which means Peter)' (Jn 1:42). Infinite love has set its eyes upon Simon and life will never be the same. He is given a new name, Peter or Cephas – meaning the rock – indicating what his life's work is to be.

So what does Jesus see? First he sees Simon, the impetuous son of John, at one moment displaying great enthusiasm, at another scepticism and even despair. But he also sees the rock. Jesus discerns that within Peter, or Cephas, are great wells of courage and loyalty that will prompt him to protestations of undying allegiance and to impromptu actions that his companions can only gape at. However, the shadow side of these great gifts will lead him into panic, denial and searing regret. He will have occasional moments of brilliance and flashes of divine inspiration. But Jesus also knows the Simon in him, he knows his human frailties, and he doesn't give up on him. Even on the night before his death, listening to Peter's protestations of undying allegiance, and knowing what awaits him and that Peter and the others will cave under the fear, pressure and anguish, Jesus addresses him by his old name, indicating that he 'sees' what is going to happen: 'Simon, Simon, Satan has asked to have all of you, to sift you like wheat. But I have pleaded in prayer for you, Simon, that your faith should not fail.' There is a sense in which he has to know himself as Simon before he can fully pick up the mantle of Peter. 'Peter' is born and grows out of the stumbling and testing of Simon, son of John. It is a journey that will last all his life, even to the point where he is an old man who will stretch out his hands and others will direct him to take him where he does not want to go. He never fully 'knows'. There's always more.

Simon, son of John, and Ruth, daughter of Tom, are every man and every woman. For many of us – perhaps we don't even remember when or how – Jesus has touched our lives at some stage, beginning a journey that will last the rest of our days. It may have been a very specific encounter or it may have been a gradual dawning awareness, but, whatever it was, the Way chose us. We have made our declaration about who Jesus is and he, in essence, gives us a new name, a new vision, a new purpose. He calls us, commissions us, to be bearers of Good News. Peter and others like him, including you and me, become the rock foundation upon which Jesus builds his Church. Peter tripped up many times and so do we, but Jesus sees the heart. He honours the heart's desire and sees the rock foundation even when we can't. Like Peter, we alternate between being enthusiastic and sceptical or even despairing. We can show great courage and loyalty, but we too have our shadow side, so often characterised by fear and denial, if not in our words then by our actions, or lack of them. We may also have our moments of brilliance and our flashes of divine inspiration, but the bottom line for us is, as it was for Simon Peter, that we love Jesus, perhaps with a similar degree of awe and earthiness as he did.

Approximately three years later, in an earth-stopping moment, Jesus again looks intently at Peter. Peter has been on a rather steep learning curve regarding his pilgrimage of faith and has stated in various ways that his loyalty and love are unshakable. Then come Jesus' arrest and trial. The combination of courage and fear draw Peter to the high priest's courtyard, where he denies the One he loves and the rooster crows. Jesus turns and looks at him, and he remembers: 'Before the rooster crows tomorrow morning, you will deny three times that you even know me.' The rock is shattered. 'Some foundation you are, Peter! To choose you is like choosing to build my church on sand. At the first storm it fell and what a great fall it was!' Do you think that was what the look Jesus gave Peter indicated? I don't. That look was, yet again, the gaze of love, a gaze that said, 'I understand'. It was that look that caused Peter to go out and weep. He was broken in a way that he had never experienced before. However, at the same time as he thought he had irrevocably damaged things, he also knew that though he didn't know much about anything anymore, especially about Jesus, his life would forever be inextricably bound up with his.

If you have ever been in a situation where everything has been stripped away from you and you feel naked, betrayed, achingly lonely and misunderstood, when all you have hoped for seems to be reduced to rubble, and all of it is compounded by the fact that you were at least partly responsible, then you will know something of how Peter felt. As mentioned earlier, in a situation like this, the one freedom left is the freedom to choose how you react. Is it with bitterness or despair as you let the tidal wave of defeat or remorse sweep over you? Or do you choose to turn and see the gaze of love from the God who knows and loves you still? That's very hard when you are bleeding inside. It seems almost impossible when you are in what feels like uncharted territory, in a dark place with no light. It might be a paradox, but, in retrospect, we can be overwhelmingly grateful for our equivalent of the rooster crowing. It is a part of our past that we must address so that we may move forward to a new day. Our lives, thank God, are not totally defined by the Simon, the smaller self, within us. There is also Cephas, Peter, the rock that can only be discovered when we allow ourselves to be still. When we let go of thinking, we can simply consent to God's presence and action within.

Within a very short space of time there are five identifiable new disciples who are committed to accompanying Jesus. Each new 'recruit' responds to the invitation 'Come and see!' Nathanael is no exception. He was a man of integrity, a seeker, maybe even a bit of a scholar. He, like so many of his contemporaries, yearned for the coming of the Messiah and for the glory of God to be manifest once again, chiefly in the liberation of his country from foreign occupation and oppression, but also in a restoration of faith. How his heart must have leapt when his friend Philip came running, breathless in his haste and excitement, to deliver the incredible news, 'We've found him! We've found the very person Moses and the prophets wrote about!' But his hopes were immediately dashed when Philip continued with, 'His name is Jesus, the son of Joseph from Nazareth.' Nathanael had a low opinion of Nazareth. Perhaps he had had a negative experience there, or there was some sort of prejudice, rivalry or jealousy between the two communities. Besides, nowhere in the scriptures did it say that the Messiah would come from Nazareth. Philip, very wisely, did not argue but instead issued the invitation, 'Come and see'.

It is so easy to write people off because of their background or birthplace. We can label and dismiss those who differ from us and, in doing so, deny ourselves the riches they might have shared with us, as well as preventing them from realising their full potential. When we think we know a person fully, we don't allow room for growth or change. 'Can any good thing come from Nazareth?' is the kind of dismissive question we hear asked of poorer townlands and communities today. After Nathanael's initial scepticism, there follows an encounter that leads us into mystery and awareness. Before they physically meet, with the gaze of love Jesus sees and knows Nathanael in his essence. Nathanael surrenders, all his arguments and prejudice dissolving like the dust on the road beneath his feet. Nathanael now knows in a place beyond all formal knowing, in a way that all his study and debating could not have led him, that he stands in the presence of 'I Am'. He lets go of all preconceived notions, even some dearly held convictions, and makes his simple, yet profound declaration, 'You are the Son of God, the King of Israel!' Jesus responds, 'Do you believe just because I said I saw you under the fig tree, Nathanael? You haven't seen anything yet. Before this is over you're going to see heaven open and the angels of God ascending and descending upon the Son of Man.' For Nathanael, and for all, the heavens have opened. Jesus, the word made flesh, is here and is the gate to life, freedom, hope, truth and love. Nothing can ever be the same again after this revelation. This is the fulfilment of Jacob's dream centuries before when, at Bethel, he saw a ladder reaching from earth to heaven and the angels of God ascending and descending upon it. What Jacob saw was a mere shadow compared to this.

Today we are living in this new dispensation, which is as fresh, as real, as hope-filled as it was for Nathanael all those years ago. It is always in the present moment that we are called to be aware. Yet the naked truth is that so often we are asleep. We are missing out on so much. When did you last stand in wonder, silent before a breathtaking sunset, sensing the love of the Creator behind it all? When were you last speechless before the beauty and the wisdom of an elderly 'saint' who communicated beyond words something of the loving presence of the I Am? When were you last on tiptoe in a building or a place made holy by the prayers of the ages so that the very stones breathed the name and the presence of God? When did you last kneel before great love and great suffering as you watched the pain and anguish of the modern world and knew that you were witnessing a silent prayer? As we yield to the process of letting go, of waking up, of becoming sensitive to the whispers behind the clamour of living, we will gradually be surprised by the joy and the awe of awareness. Francis Thompson captures this sense in his poem:

> *O world invisible, we view thee,*
> *O world intangible, we touch thee,*
> *O world unknowable, we know thee,*
> *Inapprehensible, we clutch thee! ...*

> *The angels keep their ancient places –*
> *Turn but a stone and start a wing!*
> *'Tis ye, 'tis your estrangèd faces,*
> *That miss the many-splendored thing.*[1]

In our lack of awareness, our shuttered hearts and estranged faces have missed so much; we have missed the many-splendoured thing. But because of heaven opening, because of the life, death and Resurrection of Jesus, because of the passionate love of God that we live again through the seasons of the Christian year, the truth is that we can view the invisible, touch the intangible, know the unknowable. We can do it if we are prepared to let go and simply rest under the gaze of love, realising in that very moment that we too are seen, touched and known by infinite love. We become aware that we do not have to keep straining our eyes upwards to the stars and the vastness of the universe in an attempt to draw nearer to God or catch a glimpse of an angel's wing. All about us are whispers of the infinite, vestiges of heaven. And Bethel, the House of God, is not some remote, faraway place but is found within each one of us as we become conscious of his presence and sense the first stirrings of a mutual abiding. We could echo Jacob's cry 'Surely the Lord is in this place – this inner place – and I did not know it!' This is such an exciting journey to be on. Did we think that we had discovered all there was to know about believing, about being a companion of Jesus? Like Nathanael, we haven't seen anything yet. The invitation as always is 'Come and see!'

NOTE

1. Francis Thompson, 'The Kingdom of God "In No Strange Land"', *The New Oxford Book of Christian Verse*, chosen and edited by Donald Davie (Oxford: Oxford University Press, 1985), p. 256.

CHAPTER EIGHT

A SEARCH REWARDED
(John 4:1-42)

Perhaps no encounter in the New Testament is better known and loved than that which took place at Jacob's Well near the little town of Sychar in Samaria. Jesus was on his way back to Galilee from Judea. There had been rumours spread by the Pharisees that Jesus was baptising more disciples than John the Baptist. Actually, Jesus didn't baptise anyone – his disciples did. Jesus wasn't into competition or confrontation, so he decided to go back to his home territory of Galilee. There were two possible routes back but we read that he 'had to go through Samaria'. Eventually he came near the Samaritan village of Sychar. Jacob's Well was situated at the meeting point of several ancient Roman roads, so it would have been a resting place for travellers, maybe also a place of pilgrimage. The route led through difficult terrain and was about twenty miles long. It is as if the whole story of God's dealings with his people to date converge at this moment in time, in this particular place with this significant encounter. It is a symbol of the healing, both of individual and ancient historical hurts, and of the unity, the relationship, the life-giving nourishment that Jesus comes to bring.

The Samaritans and the Jews had been bitter enemies for about seven hundred years. While they worshipped the same God, the Samaritans only used the first five books of the Old Testament as their scriptures, while the Jews also considered the writings of the prophets as sacred. The Samaritans had their own temple at Mount Gerizim, while the Jews had theirs in Jerusalem. With their sense of superiority as being truly the chosen people, the Jews despised the Samaritans. So why did Jesus, a Jew, choose the road less travelled, the more dangerous one, when he could just as easily have taken the more familiar route? In doing so, he would have been steeped in the history that surrounded him. He would have carried with him, in his historical memory as a Jew, the wounds of a divided country and an awareness of all the bitter arguments and wars over the centuries between these two small parcels of earth. However, the key religious questions and the political stances of the day did not really interest Jesus. It is likely he 'had' to come this way because he was thirsty. Physically he was tired and thirsty, but his real thirst was for something deeper. It was a yearning for communion, for unity, to bring people together, to break down the walls that separated them, to get them to meet each other, to listen to each other and to build relationship, and, beyond all of that, to find or be found again by a God who wanted to live within them. Jesus wanted, and still wants, nothing less than transformation for them and for us.

And so, near the border of a divided country, a man and a woman meet. Every conceivable barrier should have existed between them – politics, religion, culture, tradition, gender. There should have been a dividing wall of resentment, bitterness, bigotry and such irreconcilable differences that they could not even see each other. But this was no ordinary meeting. Their encounter is one of a deeper 'seeing' of each other. The woman is a lonely, wounded and marginalised person. She has lived through five broken relationships, and has experienced rejection, humiliation, worthlessness and ostracism. It is midday, the time of absence, of total aloneness – the time, later, when Jesus would be crucified. No one goes to get water at that time. It is too hot. The woman can go and not be noticed, not have to be subjected to the snide remarks that would have been commonplace had she gone at a busier time. So she comes with her water pot, not expecting anything. It is just another day, like any other. She too is thirsty for something that Jacob's Well cannot give her. There, surprisingly, she meets a stranger, a Jew, on his own. (His disciples had gone on into town to buy food.) He is thirsty. He asks her for a drink. He puts her at ease. He initiates the conversation and deliberately becomes the needy one, asking for help. He understands her. With the gaze of love he sees and knows her brokenness and he enters into relationship with her through declaring his own need. Jolted by the shock of being addressed by a male, a Jew, someone who would have known the sort of woman she was because of the timing of her trip, she is intrigued. She has no expectations of this encounter, so she can be more authentically herself. She has nothing to hide from this stranger.

Here is where it gets interesting. Most of us, when we read this account, probably go along with the traditional assumptions of a woman despised, with no education, her life experience limited by the position and opportunities of women of the day, someone who was cast aside by society because of her assumed loose morals. However, when you actually examine the exchange between the woman and Jesus, this is no uneducated, unthinking human being. She could not have entered into the dialogue she had with Jesus unless she had already been on an interior journey of her own. Jesus clearly sees something in her from the beginning, not just her wounds and their causes. He sees someone created in the image and likeness of God, as all of us are. He sees someone to whom life has dealt harsh blows, some of which she has been responsible for, some not. As already mentioned, the woman had had five husbands prior to this meeting. In those days a man was allowed to divorce a woman on the very slightest provocation. Here was a free spirit whose questions and search for meaning in life had probably exasperated the men with whom she lived! Women were not supposed to think for themselves. They were often regarded as less than slaves, and they were the water carriers. Is it any wonder such men would seek divorce if she did not keep her place, if she disturbed their peace by thinking, and by asking for something more? Perhaps, after five partners, she just gave up. Women in those days needed the protection of men, but this time she did not go for marriage. What was the point? There were no answers to her questions; life was just something to be endured, a life littered with broken relationships that had wounded her deeply and held out no promise of restoration or transformation. That is, until this particular day, this particular time and this particular encounter.

A conversation begins around the subject of water. Jesus gradually shares with her that there is another type of water that will take away thirst altogether, as it will become, in those who drink it, a perpetual spring, welling up into the life of God. She doesn't quite grasp what he is saying, but because trust is growing in her she is beginning to know herself as 'someone' again, as a human being, worthy of respect and of a place in the community, capable of doing beautiful things. Some of her confidence returns and she enters fully into what Jesus is saying. She knows in a place beyond formal knowing. Jesus doesn't have to spell it out. Cynthia Bourgeault writes, 'He sees who she is; she sees who he is. And in the light of that mutual recognition they keep on empowering each other and drawing each other along to a greater self-disclosure.'[1] It is at this point that Jesus, with deep compassion and unwavering accuracy, is able to put his finger on the deep wound of the woman, the source of her thirst. She is then able to receive it because she now understands, maybe for the first time in her life, that she is precious, respected and beloved. The process of transformation has begun and continues as she pursues another stumbling block, namely who's right and who's wrong in terms of their places of worship and their religious traditions. Jesus, in essence tells her, 'That's not important. What is important is that people worship God in spirit and in truth.'

There then comes the awesome moment of revelation and of recognition. This woman – despised, rejected, considered of no account in the eyes of her world – is the one to whom Jesus chooses to reveal his secret. He tells her that he is the Messiah, the one for whom both Jews and Samaritans have been waiting for so long. 'I am,' he says, 'I am he.' This is the first time in this Gospel that Jesus reveals his true identity to anyone. It wasn't to his disciples, those who knew him (or thought they did), or to Nicodemus, the respected teacher, but to a Samaritan woman of doubtful morals. A trust and a deep knowing has been awakened between them – she knows she has finally found that for which she had been searching for so long; he knows that here is someone who has grasped the why of his coming. How that knowing must have gladdened Jesus' heart, feeding his tired spirit and quenching some of the thirst within his being – that thirst for someone to see, to understand. It happens from within and from a great depth. Psalm 42 explains that, 'Deep calls unto deep, the sound of many waters.' It is a moment of huge significance and awareness. The depths within each person at the well make a heart-to-heart connection.

At this point, the disciples return with food. They have not yet been fully liberated from the narrow confines of their culture and are shocked at the sight of Jesus talking with a woman. Yet something holds them back from asking him why or what they had been discussing. Perhaps somewhere on the fringes of consciousness, they too are sensing something – that this is a moment of vital significance, though they cannot say why. The woman has undergone a transformation. She now knows herself as both broken and beloved; she has been given back her uniqueness and preciousness. She who had been an embarrassment, an outsider, perhaps even a curse, now becomes a blessing. She becomes the first announcer of the Good News, leaving her water jar behind – the symbol of her old life. That which has held her back is left at the feet of Jesus and she is able to run back to her own community as a witness. Her search has been rewarded. She is now vitally connected, both to her true self and to the God she has met. She is immersed in the flow. The living water wells up within her, flowing through her to the community. It must be shining from her because the villagers take note. The gaze of love she received goes with her. They don't ignore her. They listen to her story, her witness, and then decide to go and see for themselves. The people of Sychar flock to see Jesus, and he stays with them for a couple of days. They too are transformed; their thirst is quenched first by the woman's witness and then by the presence of Jesus himself.

This meeting of Jesus and the woman at Jacob's Well is a sacrament of encounter par excellence. They meet unexpectedly (certainly on the woman's part) and the ensuing engagement becomes a source of life for both of them. The woman is enabled to claim her true humanity and identity. She becomes fully herself in the light of what she is being given to see. She is drawn deeply into Jesus' life and is empowered to follow his path. She is transformed. But Jesus too receives something. He is encouraged by the depth of the encounter to say, for the first time, who he is. It is declared, and he has taken another step towards self-emptying from which there is no turning back.

John's Gospel is known as the Gospel of Signs. The events are deliberately recorded to point to Jesus' true identity. The first sign is the wedding at Cana in Galilee. The second sign is thought to be the healing of the official's son immediately after this encounter, when Jesus and his disciples return to Galilee. It seems to me that this meeting at the well and the subsequent transformation should certainly rank among the signs – perhaps even being the most important one. For this story is not only about an individual and her quest for life. It is also about a whole community, whose communal life is transformed because one person was true to her journey. So many people on the island of Ireland, being true to their journey, have taken the news of living water to the far corners of the earth, and I can only stand in awe of such a witness and commitment. From personal experience, they know that the living water was not just for the Samaritan woman or even for the villagers of Sychar, but for countless others over the centuries who would believe and be transformed because of their testimony. This was why Jesus had to go through Samaria.

Judea and Samaria remind me somewhat of Ireland, north and south. We are such a small piece of earth, yet over centuries we have been at loggerheads with each other, in both church and state. So many barriers have existed between us and, if we scratch the surface even today, after so much peace building has been done, we would still find deep-seated hostility and suspicion in politics and in religion. We have seen much change but I would question how much transformation there has been. We have things to do and places to go for God on this island, and in parts of the world we've never been to before, and we have got to go together. We also have places to go inside of ourselves that we have never been to before in order that we may be part of the shining company, bearers of the Good News, as the Samaritan woman was. I always wished she had a name and, one day, I discovered that tradition has given her a name. It is Photine, which means the luminous one. In fact, in early tradition she was numbered among the apostles and was a shining witness to the transformation, the new life that Jesus brought. She would have had no idea about her destiny when she came to Jacob's Well that day, no idea of the bigger thing God had planned.

We have no idea of God's bigger plan, but our part is vital in it. If we don't allow that transforming process to take place within us, if we do not have the faith or courage to run back to our neighbours with the one message, something else will slip. We, as the people of God in Ireland, will have missed our moment. It seems to me that, as Jesus said to the disciples when they returned from Sychar, that we have only to look, as he did with the gaze of love, to really be aware. We will see that the fields are ripening all around us and are now ready for the harvest. It will be the harvest of those who have thirsted for real life, to know that we are beloved, that we matter and that we will find the living water. We will have our thirst quenched as we take the risk not to preach at them but to enter the flow ourselves and become a conduit to this island and the world. There is only one way home. It leads neither to Jerusalem nor Gerizim. The way is not a road but a person, the person of Jesus who is still thirsting for communion, for unity for peace. His passion still is that we discover ever more deeply our thirst for him. When we risk that sort of encounter, we too will become undeniable witnesses in our communities. We too will become luminous ones. People encountering us will know that we have found water, that we have found Christ, that we have experienced the place of meeting, of reconciliation, of understanding, of unity, that our search has been rewarded. We have rested under the gaze of love and life will never be the same.

NOTE

1. Cynthia Bourgeault, *The Wisdom Jesus* (Boston, Massachusetts: Shambala Publications, 2008), p. 11.

%

CHAPTER NINE

FOUND BY THE GAZE
OF LOVE
(John 5:1-15)

While God is not confined to specific areas, there are certain places that we can identify as thin places. These are spots where our spirits stand on tiptoe with expectancy because we feel that, at any moment, the real but unseen world will break into our existence with special grace – be that with a sense of the holy, or with peace in the midst of an inner storm or even, at times, with healing. The Grotto at Lourdes is one such place, as is the old church at Knock, County Mayo, or the Abbey on the island of Iona. A few years ago I happened on another place in Switzerland. A friend and I took a boat trip on a lake to the island of Reichenau where there was an old deserted monastery. It is known locally as 'the island where the monks practised brotherhood'. And the lake, Untersee, which feeds the River Rhine, is known as the Lake of Grace. The sense of community, Presence and the sacred were very strong, almost tangible here. What makes these, and many others sites, places of Presence, I believe, is all the prayers uttered over centuries and the faithful witness of those who have gone before. Something of this has seeped into the very stones and the fabric of the buildings, and they become threshold places. Perhaps the Pool of Bethesda was one such place.

Bethesda means House of Mercy. Some call it Bethzatha, which means House of the Olive. I prefer to think of it as the former, since what those who gathered around it needed most was mercy. Beneath the pool was a subterranean stream that used to bubble up every now and then, agitating the water. The common belief, probably a superstition, was that an angel caused the disturbance, and the first person to enter the pool after the stirring of the waters would be healed of whatever disease was afflicting them. This is not so different from Irish holy wells, or even from the baths at Lourdes or any place of pilgrimage. It certainly had great power, not least for the man in this story. We are not told his name, only that he has been lying paralysed and without hope in the same place with countless others for thirty-eight years. He had lost his identity and faded into anonymity. His only name, like so many people today, is a number – Number 38. Perhaps he had been optimistic once, believing that someday he would make it into the pool first; he would be healed and life for him would change dramatically. Now it is just wishful thinking. Long ago, any flicker of hope that the healing water would stir for him had died. No one belongs to him, no care attendant, no one who could help him get into the water at the crucial time. He has been waiting for thirty-eight years and there has been no one to give him that vital shove!

This particular day is no different from any of the other interminable days. It is festival time in Jerusalem and the city is crowded; there are throngs of people everywhere. The porches around the Pool of Bethesda are packed with sick people, more than usual because of the holiday: the blind, the lame, the diseased, the paralysed, and, among them, Number 38. Jesus has come to Jerusalem for this holy day. Already he is making a name for himself as a healer and teacher and is arousing the suspicion and antagonism of the powers that be – the religious leaders of the day. As so often happens in his ministry, Jesus gravitates towards those who need him the most. He moves through the throng of needy people and, with a definite purpose in mind, stops in front of Number 38 and singles him out. It is as if he already knows his story and and has come through the Sheep Gate (referenced in John 5:2) to the Pool of Bethesda specifically to meet with him. You can imagine Number 38, lying on his mat, only half conscious of the crowds swirling around him – the noise of many voices, including street vendors and tourists. From his prostrate position all he can see are the feet of people passing by. Then, suddenly, a pair of feet stop right in front of him. He becomes aware of stillness and peace. All the noise fades into the background and it is as if there are only two people in the entire world – Number 38 and the owner of the sandaled feet. Then the unthinkable happens. Whoever has stopped is noticing him. He is addressing him, not as a number, another statistic, but as a human being. Not only this, but he asks him a question! As the words filter down through his mystified haze of consciousness, Number 38 becomes aware that the question seems to be a ridiculous one: 'Do you want to be healed? Would you like to get well?' Anybody in their right mind should know that he would love to be walking around, going about his business rather than lying here day after day. Is this person taunting him, or asking such a question because he cannot think of anything else to say? Number 38 is so conditioned in his thinking that he presumes there is only one way to get well – by getting into that pool when the water is agitated. He immediately responds by explaining to the stranger how impossible this is. 'I can't, sir, for I have no one to help me into the pool when the water is stirred up. While I am trying to get there, someone else always gets in ahead of me.'

Can you sense the desperate loneliness of this man, his isolation, his despair, the sense of defeat and negativity, bordering on self-pity? He certainly does not expect what comes next – not an expression of sympathy, or even an offer of help to get him into the water, but a quiet and authoritative command: 'Stand up, pick up your mat and walk.' Immediately the man does just that. The gaze of love has found him; the Mercy Giver has spoken the life-giving word. The man's inner being can do nothing but respond in the way he is directed. He hardly sees the face of the One who has restored him to living before the crowd swallows them both up. Number 38, a nobody no longer, but someone who, having been found by the gaze of love, now knows that he matters. With his sleeping mat rolled up under his arm, he makes his way from the pool to start his new life. He is so overwhelmed by what has happened to him that he forgets that it is the Sabbath.

There were so many rules and regulations governing what could and could not be done on the Sabbath. Apparently, if someone was caught intentionally carrying anything from a public place to a private house on the Sabbath, this 'offence' was punishable by death by stoning. Up until a few years ago we might have thought, 'How ridiculous! That would never happen today.' However, looking at the atrocities committed by militant extremists, we can see that human nature actually hasn't changed very much, certainly in terms of what happens when people become fanatical about their religion and the multitudinous laws governing it.

The man, probably still stunned by the miracle of what has happened to him, is oblivious of what day it is. He is stopped by the authorities who accuse him of breaking the law. This seems strange to me. Here is a man whom I'm sure they recognised;

he'd been ill or paralysed for so many years and was always lying in the same spot, and now he is walking as well as any of them! They don't ask him how this happened. A miracle of healing does not seem to even register with them. All they can see is someone who is breaking one of their man-made rules. The man, somewhat bemused, replies, 'The man who healed me said to me, "Pick up your sleeping mat and walk".' They want to know who it is, although they probably have an inkling if they have had their ears to the ground. The man says he does not know. Later, Jesus finds him in the temple. The gaze of love searches him out yet again. I find this so moving. It is almost a second healing, as if there has been some unfinished business. Saint John does not say Jesus bumped into him but, rather, Jesus found him; he must have been looking for him specifically. 'Now you are well; so stop sinning, or something even worse may happen to you.'

At first reading this statement may sound like a threat, which is not very Jesus-like! We don't know anything about this man's history, but probably the biggest sin we commit (and possibly this was his sin also) is not accepting the fact of our own belovedness. From that unacceptance and disbelief, many negative thoughts and attitudes can arise, some of which can lead to illness and disease. Negative, even violent behaviour can also be the outcome of a life that has never awakened to the fact that it is accepted, loved and beautiful. This was the main reason God came in the person of Jesus – not to judge and condemn, but to reveal to humankind that we are all beautiful and beloved, broken, yes, but also loved. This was the newfound dignity, self-respect and worth that the man carried with him, as well as his sleeping mat, on that eventful day. He was standing up, both on the outside and the inside, and Jesus was saying, 'Don't lose this. Don't doubt it. Keep on walking and don't slip back into the trap you were in before.' After this encounter the man goes to find the Jewish leaders to tell them that it was Jesus who had healed him. He was not seeking to get Jesus into trouble, he was merely trying to explain that it was not his fault that he had broken the law. Perhaps, somewhat naively, he thought they might welcome such a teacher and healer. What it actually does is give them further ammunition with which to harass and condemn Jesus.

Until this point of encounter with Jesus, Number 38 was merely a statistic. Examples of people being reduced to mere statistics are all too common, not least those imprisoned in concentration camps in the Second World War. Viktor Frankl was Prisoner Number 119,104 in Auschwitz. Corrie ten Boom was Number 66,730 in Ravensbrück. Both these remarkable people had been stripped of everything, but both came to recognise that they had one freedom left that no one could take away from them unless they themselves chose to surrender it – the freedom to choose how they reacted to their situation. Both of them responded to that inner voice that urged them, even in the vilest and most despairing of situations, to stand up, pick up their mat and walk. Viktor Frankl writes:

> What was really needed was a fundamental change in our attitude toward life. We had to learn ourselves and, furthermore, we had to teach the despairing men, that it did not really matter what we expected from life, but rather what life expected from us. When a man finds that it is his destiny to suffer, he will have to accept his suffering as his task; his single and unique task. His unique opportunity lies in the way in which he bears his burden.[1]

Corrie ten Boom writes:

> Life in Ravensbrück took place on two separate levels,
> mutually impossible. One, the observable, external life,
> grew every day more horrible. The other, the life we lived
> with God, grew daily better, truth upon truth, glory upon
> glory.[2]

We often readily surrender our freedom to choose. None of us, I
imagine, or very few, have had to undergo the sort of nightmare
that Viktor Frankl and Corrie ten Boom endured. However, it
is very easy and understandable to let what has happened to
us in life completely shape us. This is especially so if we have
been deeply hurt or suffered some great trauma or loss. We can
be trapped by such negativity. We feel that there is no one who
could really understand or do anything to improve the situation.
There are also many people, mainly the elderly, all around us,
living in acute loneliness, feeling like no one knows or cares
about them. They may present a different face to the outside
world, but when they are on their own, which is most of the
time, they hardly know themselves, or what once gave them
their identity or zest for living. They are also simply a number, a
statistic, like Number 38. Sometimes we can feel like that too. It
can happen because of illness, disappointment, ageing, betrayal,
or any one of a hundred losses. We all have something inside of
us that we wish was different, and we often allow it to become
the reason for our behaviour. Perhaps we have given up any
hope that things might change, and are imprisoned in a sort of
silent despair. Whatever our situation, I sometimes wonder how
we would respond if someone said to us one day, 'Do you want
to be healed? Would you like things to be different for you?' We

can't make it happen for ourselves – in that sense, the man at the Pool of Bethesda was right. However, we can cooperate when the time comes, and we need to be alert and aware so that, when it does, we do not miss it. God is the God of surprises; he does not always act in the way we think he will or even should! Do I want to be well? What do I answer? What would 'being well' mean? Sometimes when we are offered something for which we have been waiting quite some time, we become frightened. The sleeping mat can be uncomfortably 'comfortable'. To say an inner 'yes' would eventually mean a lot of outer affirmations. It would mean new responsibilities and greater demands. To truly receive the gaze of love could also mean opposition or rejection from those who still do not see and are trapped in their legalism or religion, or in their own hurt or grievance. Out of their own 'illness' or imprisonment, they are envious. They do not like to see change. Like the man at Bethesda who, from the moment of his healing, encountered opposition and curiosity, and who had never been thought worthy of notice before, being well would also mean a new sense of accountability and responsibility. To be healed, to say 'yes', is an exciting and awesome opportunity and we do right to wrestle with the question before we answer. Would we soon yearn for the security of slavery in Egypt like the Israelites long ago, or long for the sleeping mat beside the pool where no one really noticed us or expected anything of us, where we could remain in the vague half-hope that someday something might happen?

Jesus indicated that the man needed to do three things: to stand up, to pick up his sleeping mat and to walk. We face the same challenge today. What does it mean to stand up? Personally, it is about standing up inside myself, as someone who is in the process of becoming all that God has planned in his heart and mind for me from the very beginning. When I begin to tap into the mystery of my belovedness, that process becomes gloriously possible. What does it mean to pick up my sleeping mat? For me, it is about exercising my freedom to choose my response, no matter what the situation. The man at the pool was carrying the mat that had once carried him. He was no longer a prisoner of his situation. He had discovered a greater freedom. So we need to ask ourselves: 'What has my particular sleeping mat been over the years, the thing that I have allowed to control and determine how I live, and how can I now alter that way of being?' What does it mean to start walking? For me, it is about walking the talk. As people of faith, we can too readily slip into clichés or use the language of faith without actually living it. This can lead to a huge credibility gap between what we say and what we do. The only antidote that I know of is to stop sinning – to believe that nothing I can do or fail to do will make God love me more or less than he does right now in this eternity moment. We must start believing it, not some day but right now. It could be that today, as you read this, is your time, your day. You may feel and even believe that all sorts of wonderful things seem to happen for other people but not for you. Someone else always gets in before you. Today, this precious day has been given to you. Perhaps, as you go about your daily tasks, something may emerge that will be for you a pool, a place of mercy. Perhaps you will be found by the gaze of love. Perhaps, Jesus will step alongside you as if you were the only one he had come for, and ask you the question, 'Do you want to be well?'

When all else is stripped away, what will your answer be to this most searching of questions?

NOTES

1. Viktor Frankl, *Man's Search for Meaning* (London: Hodder and Stoughton, 1964), p. 77.

2. Corrie ten Boom, *The Hiding Place* (London: Hodder and Stoughton, 1973), p. 182.

※

CHAPTER TEN

THE GAZE THAT HEALS
(Luke 8:40-48)

Tradition has given her the name Veronica (meaning a true likeness). In the Gospels she is simply referred to as the woman with the haemorrhage who had been ill for twelve years. She had been to many doctors and had tried every method of healing, but nothing helped. She had spent all her savings and her condition, if anything, was worse than ever. Her situation was desperate. Not only was she ill and debilitated because of blood loss, she was also isolated. Jewish law declared that she was ceremonially unclean. So long as her haemorrhaging continued, anything she touched was regarded as defiled. We can only imagine the shame, the utter loneliness and the rejection that accompanied her condition. She must have felt unclean in body and in spirit. The life she currently lived was intolerable. Perhaps, like so many people, she didn't feel right about praying for herself. On this particular day she notices that there is more than the usual buzz about the streets of Capernaum. Alone as she is, she can still sense the excited gossip and expectancy in the crowd. Jesus from Nazareth, whose name has been on the lips of an increasing number of people because of his teaching and the miracles he performs, is crossing the lake with his friends and is about to come to shore at any moment. The woman knows deep within her being that she just has to reach him. He is her last chance.

But someone else in the crowd, someone very important, is determined to get to Jesus first because, for him also, Jesus is his only hope. This is Jairus, leader of the local synagogue, and respected member of the community. His only child, a little girl of twelve, is dying. His desperation overcomes his sense of importance and reputation in the community. He runs and falls down at Jesus' feet begging him to come and heal his daughter. The woman would have witnessed all of this and would have seen her chances of any encounter slipping away. Jairus was somebody; she was less than nobody. But her desperation also makes her bold. She does not seek a meeting with Jesus or feel worthy of it, but she has a strong sense that this is a day of destiny for her. 'If I can only get close enough to touch the fringe of his robe, I will get well. He won't even need to know I'm there.'

All devout Jewish men wore robes with fringes on them over their tunics. The fringes ended in four tassels of white thread with a blue thread woven through them. The tassels were a reminder to obey the commandments of God and the blue thread was believed to represent the Spirit. One of the traditions associated with the longed-for Messiah was that the knotted fringes of his robe possessed healing power. The woman probably knows this, so it is her desperate intention to touch one of these knotted fringes as she tries to slip through the pressing throng that swirled around Jesus. Those knowing her condition shun or verbally abuse her, so it must be very difficult to get close enough, especially as Jairus is hurrying him along. She jostles her way through, seeing nothing or nobody but Jesus. The drama of Jairus' plight diverts the attention of the crowd and, unnoticed, she reaches out, her hand coming into contact with the fringe of his robe. Immediately she knows that she is healed – the bleeding had stopped – but so do Jesus and the crowd around him. His voice rings out through babble of noise, 'Who touched me?' Everyone denies it. The disciples have been on a whirlwind journey over the previous days, witnessing things they could never have imagined: the restoring to life of a man in Nain; the calming of a fierce storm on the lake; the healing of a madman at Gerasa; and now they have been summoned by the leader of the local synagogue for help. But at this precise moment perhaps they think Jesus is losing it. Peter, as usual, voices what the others are thinking, 'Master, there's a huge crowd pressing in around you. You can't move an inch without coming into close contact with dozens of people. Everyone is touching you.' They have all stopped, and, somewhere among them is a frightened but rejoicing woman. 'No,' says Jesus in response to Peter's somewhat patronising remark, 'Someone deliberately touched me for I felt healing power leave me.'

There is silence. The people begin to look around while Jesus waits. The woman is now trembling as she knows that she can no longer remain anonymous. He is waiting for her and she has to declare herself. She moves through the crowd and falls to her knees in front of him. Again, it is as if there are just two people in all of Capernaum – Jesus and herself. She tells her story and explains why she had to touch him and how she has been instantly healed. The crowd is hanging on her every word. Jesus is deeply moved. He uses a term of endearment, 'Daughter, you took a risk trusting me. Now you are healed and whole. Your faith has made you well. Live well. Be blessed. Go in peace.' He not only wants to heal her from her physical condition but also from the rejection, isolation and shame that has clung to her for twelve years. So he calls her out in front of all the people; he affirms her as a daughter of Abraham, fully acceptable to the community; he puts his seal upon her healing;

he commends her for her faith and trust, and he releases her with a blessing. She is not only healed; she is made whole. A new life opens out in front of her. Veronica has been touched in her body, her soul and her spirit; her life belongs to the one who has healed her and set her free. Tradition tells us that she became a follower of Jesus and that it was she who, on the way to the cross, met with him in a special, anguished, loving moment and wiped his face with a towel. It is almost a reversal of roles. At a point when he could not ask for anything for himself, she came to him and touched him, for his sake.

It is probably true to say that, like Veronica, we find it easier to pray for other people than we do for ourselves. Praying for others is what we've been taught to do and what we feel we should do. Somehow our needs do not seem to be as important as theirs. We perhaps feel a bit self-centred and therefore guilty. All the while, however, our own aching need remains. Even when we feel we are in desperate need, somehow to ask others to pray for us sits better with us than going to God directly with requests for ourselves. I cannot count the number of times people have said to me, 'Please pray for me. God will listen to your prayers much more than to mine!' What a distortion of a loving God who has no favourites but hears the prayers of all his people, regardless of what rung of the ladder they feel they are on. We are all on an equal footing before God, in the place of unconditional love. God delights in us coming to him in trust and loving surrender to ask for what we need. What pains him is when we pass judgement on ourselves and count ourselves unworthy to come. None of us are worthy in that sense – even the holiest of us. We are all a broken people, but we are broken and beloved. We are daughters and sons of a loving God who wants us to take the risk of trusting him. His desire is that we be people of faith. He believes in us and trusts that we can do it.

Why do we find it so hard to trust both ourselves and God? Why do we find it so difficult to dare to reach out to the One who is already reaching out to us? Jesus said to the woman, 'Daughter, your faith has made you well.' He was acknowledging that she had crossed that particular barrier, her faith meeting his power, and the result was beyond what she ever dreamed. This is not to get embroiled in the argument as to why it is that some people get healed and others do not. We do not know why this is – it remains part of the mystery. However, whether they experience the healing they particularly desire or not, for every sincere prayer that is prayed, acknowledged or not, some shift occurs for them, some measure of peace, or healing of relationship, or renewed outlook on life, or any one of a hundred things.

I have a dear friend whom I don't see very often, but on the occasions when it is possible, I go to his door with a trust born out of experience that he will hear my knock and that there will be a welcome. When I hear his voice with the one word, 'Come!' I enter confidently knowing that there will be no credibility gap between the word and the actuality. He is there, totally present in loving awareness. Among other things, what that does for me is affirm me in my personhood, in who I am. It assures me that I am accepted without conditions attached. In such an atmosphere of mutual trust, I am set free to be real. I do not need to pretend any more that everything is 'fine' when it is not, neither do I need to mask my joy when things are going well out of fear of offending someone for whom things are not going quite so well. If that can be true on a human level, and I'm sure we all know at least one person like that, then how much more so is it true of God? The questions and the doubts are from our side, not his.

We should not feel like we are an interruption. This woman, in the eyes of the onlookers, was an interruption to the urgent summons from Jairus whose daughter was dying. In fact, she dares to be an interruption! They would have wondered why Jesus slowed down and waited when everyone around him was urging him to hurry, as he had important business to do and time was running out. However, Jesus knew what he was doing. He was totally aware and in the present. Once he sensed that someone had reached out to him with intent, he was completely attentive to the one whom others regarded as an interruption. She was not an addendum or a dehumanised parenthesis in the main story of his dealings with humankind. Yet this is the way most of us tend to read it. We are part of the group moving along with Jairus when, in an untidy way, there is a hiatus while Jesus deals with someone who wasn't part of the story in the beginning. This is the way all three of the Gospel writers tell it. Maybe with the wisdom of hindsight they were trying to get us to see, yet again, that all are equal in Jesus' sight. We have all been an essential part of the story from the very beginning. Can we believe that? If not, then why not?

Nothing ever happens quite the way we plan it. In Restoration Ministries we may be working on some project that has a deadline, or be involved in a weighty and, to our minds, vital discussion, when the telephone rings or the doorbell goes. At times it is all too easy to groan inwardly a little because what we are doing at the time seems so important. However, we have learned over the years that, in fact, the interruptions are the real work. I can think of so many occasions when what seemed like an interruption turned out to be a huge moment of grace and blessing, not only for those who called, but for us too. So now, when the telephone rings, or there is a knock at the door, we simply say to each other the important word 'hospitality'. The 'letting go' then becomes easier, and is even welcomed because we know that the present moment is both a gift and a challenge to us from God, especially if the person is someone who believes that they are not important.

It usually takes an awful lot for someone with a need to approach another person. They feel invisible. They are hesitant, fearful of being a nuisance, or worried that they are interrupting something important. I find myself feeling sad when someone says to me, 'I really wanted to see you or talk with you, but I know you are so busy!' I have to examine myself and see what it is in me that is causing the other person to feel that way. Whatever it is, I need to do something about it. While they hide behind their self-effacing and apologetic approach, I can hide behind my busyness and even feel justified if I'm being busy for God!

One of the hallmarks of a true disciple or friend of Jesus is the degree to which they are willing to be interrupted, not on a superficial level, but when the interruption is about encounter, trust and authentic meeting. The interruption on the road to Jairus' house was one such encounter. It not only blessed the woman, but Jesus as well. He rejoiced in her faith. It encouraged him on his journey. He stood with her in an act of solidarity. This encounter is a sign of the beloved community where diversity is welcomed, where the margins become the centre, where the invisible become visible, and where the meaning of being the people of God is challenged and stretched.

Sometimes those who are suffering greatly do not need more words. They have had enough of those. When trying to help, the temptation can be to say something, often too much, because we feel that is what they expect, or maybe even what we expect from ourselves. We can fall into the trap of 'How am I doing in this situation?' rather than being sensitive and noticing how they are doing. What they do need is a loving and accepting presence. In truth, it is the Spirit of God within to which they are reaching out; in our mutual brokenness we are both blessed. In that understanding, not of the mind but of the heart, that 'standing under' and acknowledging the mystery of pain, a healing power begins to flow. People do not necessarily want answers so much as an acknowledgment that they have been heard, and that somebody is standing with them in an act of loving solidarity.

If the tradition is right, the things that characterised Veronica's life in the beginning were further enhanced as she became a follower of Jesus. It was a similar type of courage that prompted her to push through the crowds that day in Capernaum, later enabling her to brave the Roman guard and the restless mob baying for blood in order to reach Jesus in loving compassion on his way to the cross. We can practise this every day, in some way or other, so that our courage, ability and trust to be fully in the present moment is enhanced. For the friends of Jesus, when we practise a mode of being, then the 'invisible' become visible, the despairing become hopeful, the silent are given voice, the ostracised are embraced as part of community, and the diseased are given rest and peace. They are blessed – we are blessed – and the heart of God rejoices.

SEARCHED OUT
AND RECOGNISED
BY THE GAZE OF LOVE

✣

CHAPTER ELEVEN

THROUGH THE LENS OF LOVE
(Mark 10:17-31)

At the time of writing I am staying at a retreat centre run by the Society of African Missions, in the heart of County Down. Here I find a welcoming bolthole from the demands of day-to-day living. It is nearly the end of June and the summer, that has been late in coming, appears to be making up for lost time. All around are shrubs and blooms of every kind, the flowers lifting their heads to the sun that has been 'absent without leave' for far too long. The colours stun one into silence. Ancient trees lift their branches as if to touch a clear blue sky. The lake shimmers in the stillness, its surface rippling only slightly as two swans, lifelong companions and guardians of this stretch of water, cross and re-cross their territory like sentries on guard duty. They do it so gracefully. All this is accompanied by a symphony, starting with the dawn chorus or reveille and continuing on a more muted note throughout the day until nature's last post is sounded. Then the sun streaks the sky with tints of glorious rose and red. The world is still, at least for the moment, for there is a silent retreat in progress. People have come out of the noise of their lives, seeking to pause in the still point in their turning world and to rest in the gaze of love.

Dromantine, the name of this centre, is a place where I love to walk. Being a driven person, the temptation for me is to see how many circuits of the lake I can do before coming back to study. This could easily become an obsession so that I no longer 'see' the beauty or 'hear' the sounds of silence, since my overriding aim is to clock up the miles. This time, however, I do not have a choice. I have pulled a muscle in my back so that it is impossible for me to walk quickly. In fact, one circuit is more than enough. This morning I walked slowly. Instead of fretting over the shorter distance covered, I allowed myself to pause and be absorbed by my surroundings. I became aware that all of the beauty around me existed for one purpose only – to bring glory to God.

Today it seemed to me that each living thing accepted, without reservation, what they were. Out of that freedom, they could abandon themselves to being the most luxuriant rhododendron bush, the most fragrant rose, the most expansive tree, the most rambling honeysuckle they could be. As I listened to the bird song I remembered an old proverb: 'A bird does not sing to bring up the dawn. It sings because the dawn is coming.' All of this is the antithesis of the way we, as humankind, tend to live our lives. We are not at ease with who we are. We want to be somebody else. We are dissatisfied with, for example, our physical appearance, our work, our possessions, our personalities; the grass is always greener on the other side. We are worried about many things. Instead of accepting ourselves, we think that everything would improve if only our circumstances would change. We sing to try to bring up the dawn without recognising that it is just wasted effort. What will it take for us to change direction, to trust that the dawn is coming without any forcing on our part, to believe what we have to offer in the totality of who we are is accepted, respected, loved? Is it too risky, too frightening to press the pause button and become aware of the gaze of love from the One who waits with infinite patience and tenderness for us to awaken?

During his three years of public ministry, Jesus was an itinerant preacher. There were those who would have liked to accompany him, but when they heard about his lifestyle they turned away. 'Foxes have dens to live in, and birds have nests, but I, the Son of Man, have no home of my own, not even a place to lay my head,' he once said to a would-be follower, of whom we hear no more. On one occasion, just as he was setting out on yet another journey, a man came running up to him and knelt down before him. The disciples and other followers of Jesus would have been thronging around, but, at this man's approach fell back, as we tend to do in the presence of the rich and powerful, as if their worldly goods give them an instant rite of passage to whatever they are seeking. We are not told his name or even his age, yet tradition knows him as the rich young ruler. He seemed to have everything going for him. He had led a moral, upright life. He was respectful and well mannered. He was rich and successful, probably the pride and joy of his parents.

However, he wanted more. He wanted something he knew money could not buy. He had heard of Jesus and something within him stirred as if recognising that he could be the one who had the answers for what he sought. In deference, he kneels before Jesus and asks the question, confident that he will receive the answer to his seeking. 'Good Teacher, what should I do to get eternal life?' There is a pause. Then Jesus speaks and his first comment is not what was expected. Perhaps it was insincere flattery or a genuine recognition that prompted the young man to preface his question with 'Good Teacher'. Perhaps he was hoping that Jesus would say, 'You're doing so well. You've covered everything.' Jesus, however, begins with what is almost a rebuke, reminding his hearers that only God deserves the title 'good'. Then he adds, 'But as for your question – you know the answer already.' He lists off the commandments and perhaps the young man experiences a sigh of relief that he is measuring up. Or perhaps there is still a nagging uncertainty that he is not doing enough and there must be something more. Still on his knees, he responds, 'Teacher, I am already doing all that. In fact I have obeyed all the commandments since I was a child.'

What follows can only be described as a holy pause. There is a silence as if all of creation is listening. Jesus sees beyond all the exterior trappings. He sees the young man through the lens of love, penetrating right to his core. Mark tells us that Jesus looked at him with love. This is the only encounter in the four Gospels where this is spelled out so directly. The gaze of Jesus on those he met was always that of love, but there must have been something especially engaging about this young man for it to be recorded so unequivocally. After the look comes the challenge, the bottom line. 'You lack only one thing.' The young man is poised to hear. Surely whatever is asked, he will be able to do. 'Go and sell all you have and give the money to the poor, and you will have treasure in heaven. Then come and follow me.' There is another pause, another silence. The body language says it all. The young man's face falls. He gets up from his knees and turns away full of sadness because 'he had great possessions'. This time he is not running, but departing slowly and heavily with the burden of his choice. The gaze of love follows him until he disappears from view. He exits the pages of scripture and we do not hear of him again.

The young man is not the only one to experience sadness. I imagine Jesus too was sorrowful. Here was someone ideally suited for discipleship, someone who would have added greatly to the team. There was only one thing missing. Jesus spells it out to the crowd of followers around him, 'How hard it is for rich people to get into the Kingdom of God.' He repeats the statement, spelling it out a little bit more clearly, 'It is very hard for those who put their trust in riches to get into the Kingdom of God.' When read superficially, this encounter is seen as an indictment on those who are wealthy, a judgement on having possessions. However, this interpretation misses the point entirely. It is not those who are rich who will find it difficult to be part of the Kingdom, but those who put their trust in their riches, those who make a god out of their possessions. It is true that, for many of us, the more things we have, the more we rely on them to bring us peace, security and happiness. Unless we are aware and awake, our trust can be easily misplaced and God can be sidelined, even though we still protest our allegiance.

I am intrigued by Jesus' response, 'You lack only one thing'. It is almost identical to his response to Martha of Bethany. The young man based his sense of worth on obeying all the commandments; he would have obeyed another ten of them if he could. Yet his wealth still controlled him. He did not own great possessions – they owned him! Both Martha and the young man had the wrong end of the stick. Both were good people, worthy members of their community and their place of worship, anxious about doing the right thing. They thought that by doing more they would discover the secret of life in its fullness, when really they needed to do less. It is interesting to note that just prior to this encounter with the rich young ruler in Mark's Gospel, there is the account of Jesus blessing the children. Some mothers were keen to bring their children to him, but the disciples, acting like bodyguards, pushed them aside and told them not to bother the Teacher. But Jesus saw this – the gaze of love is always awake, vibrant, present – and was very annoyed at his would-be protectors. 'Let the children come to me. Don't stop them! The Kingdom of God belongs to such as these. I assure you, anyone who doesn't have their kind of faith will never get into the Kingdom of God.' It's as if he is setting the stage for the next encounter, one that will elaborate on what he was demonstrating when he blessed the children. Children know little of the Ten Commandments. They 'toil not, neither do they spin'. They respond in trust and innocence to the gaze of love. They are not yet owned or possessed by things. Perhaps, for an all too brief and precious time, they 'remember' from whence they came and carry with them the vestiges of that heart of love. Their faith is a surrendering in trust and love to the One who loves, without any strings attached.

The young man was posing the wrong question when he asked, 'What must I do?' It was not about doing but about being. It was about letting go of those possessions he regarded as necessary for his existence, so that he might find or be found again by the God who loved him totally. It was not about obeying more commandments or striving to keep all the rules and regulations, exercises that still left him feeling dissatisfied. It was about discovering the liberating truth that nothing he could do would make God love him more than he already did. Similarly, nothing he could do would make God love him less. We are called to be doers of the word, but when our doing arises from our being then it will be more focused and effective. It is a lesson each of us needs to learn from our own experiences. Human nature has not really changed from that day when the young seeker ran and knelt before Jesus. I heard someone who is heavily involved in philanthropic works, say in all seriousness the other day, 'I hope I'm doing enough to earn a place in heaven!' And I felt very sad because it appeared that, even after a lifetime of service, he had not discovered that there was only one thing he lacked, one thing that had nothing to do with his good works or his possessions, but focused on who he was. The 'who are you?' question intimidates many people. It is uncharted territory. They've never discovered the treasure that is them, so they busy themselves with good works. The question of what more they need to do to get eternal life becomes a constant and anxious companion. They are good people but they are not peaceful to be around, their restlessness can be disturbing and uncomfortable.

Those of us of a certain age remember a generation that, out of necessity, had to work very hard for relatively little monetary reward. Those born towards the end of World War I, their young adulthood overshadowed by World War II, were no strangers to poverty and were virtual prisoners to the Protestant work ethic. Nonetheless they had many saving graces such as a wonderful sense of humour and a great delight in getting to know different people. But as age and infirmity increase, sometimes the humour fades and strangers become more frightening. They have based their sense of worth and identity largely in their doing. When they are no longer able to 'do' there is often no time left to be introduced to the secret of being. Their generation never had time to reflect. It would have been regarded as a luxury and, perhaps, self-indulgence.

I have an elderly friend who now lives in the shadowy world of dementia. Before the shadows became impenetrable she would say over and over again, 'I'm no use any more. I don't do anything. Will I get to heaven if God sees that I'm not doing anything?' For an intelligent woman with a larger-than-life personality, someone who was always at the centre of the fun, this fear of not measuring up to some self-concocted ideal was childish, rather than childlike. She had had a very strict upbringing where conformity was demanded and where any positive attention was focused on her brother, the only son. She never felt loved or accepted just as she was. There was always something missing, which she interpreted as something lacking in her, rather than the failure of those closest to her to affirm her in her unique personhood. Certainly her image of God as infinite love, whose gaze was constantly directed at her in tenderness and delight, was totally beyond her comprehension or acceptance. Part of her, therefore, remained a child, desperately seeking assurance and acceptance, yet never convinced. During her working years she was very busy and competent, filling her leisure hours with other kinds of hectic activity, using humour and fun to mask the rejection and fear felt within. To simply 'be' held too many fears for her. However, in retirement, with her raison d'être gone, the caged monsters within could no longer be controlled. I can only trust that in her present darkness, a place that none of her friends can penetrate, the gaze of love still reaches her. I believe it does. For, as Jesus said to his followers after the encounter with the young man, 'Nothing is impossible with God.'

Perhaps my friend is an extreme example of those who base their worth totally on what they *do* rather than who they *are* – a walking, breathing, living locus of pain and anguish, hidden behind a carefully constructed facade of competence or humour or indifference. In our most honest moments many of us could identify, at least in part, with some of what they live through. It can be quite frightening to contemplate letting go of the things we regard as essential to our existence. They may have become so much a part of us that our identity is totally tied up with them. They could be our possessions, or a particular way of life, or our political or religious stance, or even a relationship. These are not bad in themselves, but can become subtle forms of idolatry. We all fall into the trap from time to time. Initially it can seem liberating and comforting, masking the urgency of the 'who are you?' question. We are lulled into the false security of doing more, but when we pause, we realise that there is still an emptiness within. We come with our question, like the rich young ruler, 'What more must I do in order to be assured of eternal welcome and hospitality?' If, at some point, we have enough courage, faith, or even desperation to pause and wait, we too may sense that we are being looked at through the lens of love. The gaze of love pinpoints the one thing lacking, namely our willingness to let go of our carefully constructed self-protection. If we wait long enough, as all heaven holds its breath, we may become aware of the identity of the one who beckons. In responding to this infinite love, we risk stepping into another world, a kingdom that is all about us and within us. We begin the journey of discovery of who we really are: beloved daughters and sons of God. Out of such awareness comes the freedom to be and to do, no longer controlled by our own agenda, but rather by God's presence and action within.

This does not happen overnight. Sometimes it feels like we are taking one step forward and two steps back as we move between the two worlds. Like any other precious gift or treasure, we need to practise being present to Presence, to the gaze of love. Peter and the others, even after being in such close contact with Jesus for some time, did not get it all at once. In fact, it took a lifetime, as it will for us, of getting it and losing it, and getting it again. It is quite salutary to note that even after Jesus' encounter with the rich young ruler, and sharing his subsequent thoughts with his disciples, Peter comes up with an almost identical question to that of the young man, simply couched in different words. As usual with Peter, he was probably only impulsively voicing what the others were thinking. He starts by mentioning all that he and the others had left behind, and then reminds Jesus that they have given up everything to follow him. The tacit question is, 'What's in it for us – after all we've done?' Perhaps we can secretly sympathise with this reaction. We are only human after all! Jesus' reply is seemingly very reassuring, 'Everyone who has "let go", who has given up what has been so dear to them for the sake of the Good News, will receive back a hundred fold.' However, in the list of blessings to be returned he adds one that could make us hesitate and feel slightly uncomfortable. The little phrase is 'and persecutions as well!' It is reminiscent of the eighth Beatitude, 'Blessed are those who are persecuted for righteousness' sake for the Kingdom of Heaven is theirs.' And just in case we haven't fully got it, he adds, 'Blessed are you when you are mocked and persecuted and lied about because you are my followers. Be happy about it! Be very glad! For a great reward awaits you in Heaven. And remember, the ancient prophets were persecuted too.'

There are very few, if any, of us who could say with total conviction, 'Bring it on, Lord! We're ready!' This is not a masochistic statement. It is not saying that to be persecuted is blessed. What it is saying is that if we have responded to the gaze of love and are numbered among the friends of Jesus, then inevitably we will come up against the enemies of such a Way. The enemies are things like greed, power seeking, control, jealousy, resentment, bitterness – those negative forces that can take root in human beings and leave devastation, destruction and despair in their wake. Perhaps the only thing that will sustain us in times like these is knowing we are held in the gaze of love, broken, yes, and beloved. In the upside-down kingdom of God, the one that is here and yet still to come, Jesus assures those who are downtrodden of their unique place. The God of surprises welcomes the last as being first and the first as being last.

'What must I do?' is a question many of us seekers repeatedly ask, even though we have been awakened to another way of being. It is so easy to slip back into the conditioned mindset of doing, perhaps because we cannot fully believe the love that is waiting, or because it is much easier to be busy than to be still. It is not either/or. It is both/and. Jesus seems to set great store by one thing in particular, namely entering into a loving relationship with God. He told many parables about it in order that we might reach a true understanding of the treasure that can be ours, that is waiting to be discovered. One of my favourites is about the merchant who was on the lookout for really wonderful pearls. When he discovered one of enormous value, he sold everything he owned and bought it. We know this story as 'The Pearl of Great Price'. This pearl, I believe, is that totally loving relationship, that communion with him that nothing can destroy. Once we become aware of it, even a little, there is no turning back. We know that all the riches in the world cannot compare with such a knowable and priceless mystery. Also, perhaps, it might give us confidence and courage for the journey to recognise that each of us is a priceless pearl to Jesus, and that we must surrender in trust and love to the One who loves us unconditionally and forever.

※

CHAPTER TWELVE

LET'S CELEBRATE
(Luke 15:11-32)

When I was a child there wasn't much money; my parents worked hard to make ends meet. However, birthdays, anniversaries and special occasions were always celebrated, even with very little. The most exciting date in the calendar was Christmas Day, when we even had Christmas crackers. The jokes in the crackers weren't all that funny, but we would laugh uproariously. The one that appeared with great regularity and always achieved the most prolonged laughter, partly because we knew the answer, was: Question: 'Who was sorriest when the prodigal son returned?' Answer: 'The fatted calf!'

A celebration is a time for letting one's hair down, for feasting, laughing, music and dancing. From earliest times, people have turned to these forms of expression whenever they wanted to mark a special occasion – a birth, a marriage, a homecoming, a coming of age. It was important in lives that were otherwise rather drab to enjoy the sights, smells, colours and sounds of celebration at key points. Many cultures also 'celebrate' at funerals, perhaps with more tears than laughter, but still with the feast, the music, the storytelling and even the dancing. I asked a friend from Nigeria, 'Why do Africans dance so much, even at funerals?' The answer was that they were celebrating that the person had gone to a better life and that their suffering was over. The dance was about life, about celebrating the person and purging the emotions that surrounded the parting. Throughout the ages, people from every race seem to have a fascination with dance. It is as if the dance expresses what is deepest within them, something that they do not feel free to communicate in any other way. There is a Burundi proverb that states, 'The one who beats the drum gives out the rhythm for the dance. The one who is at the top determines who beats the drum.' For me, that is a profoundly spiritual insight. Apart from the continent of Africa, however, where dancing is as natural as breathing and the rhythm of the dance is in perfect synchronisation with the heartbeat of the people, most of us are spectators rather than participants. We are avid spectators, perhaps because in the dance, done well, we sense an elemental freedom for which we long but fear may never again be ours.

Ever since I can remember – ever since I became aware of the gift of imagination – my image of inner freedom has been that of a dancing spirit. The outer manifestation of this has yet to emerge. When I try to dance, however, I feel as if I have two left feet! This does not stem from having no rhythm in my being, nor from any insensitivity to music; in fact quite the opposite. But I lack the confidence to surrender myself to them. I have heard the distant drum and I know from where the rhythm comes. For various reasons, nature and nurture among them, I cannot quite master the dance. The beat, the heartbeat, is love. Why do I resist? For I know that to get lost in the dance is to get lost in God, which is really to be found by him.

Sometimes we can fall into the trap of thinking that we live in an age of such enlightenment and advanced knowledge. On one level that is true, but at another level we're really only at kindergarten stage. In the early centuries of Christianity, when scholars were trying to explain the nature of God, they used a Greek word *perichoresis*, which meant dancing. All these centuries later we are only now being reawakened to such a knowable mystery. The ancient scholars did not say that God, Father, Son and Holy Spirit was *like* a dance, but that God was the dance itself. This indicates a movement, a flow, a vital relationship, into which we, as the beloved of his heart, are also invited. How do we pick up the rhythm of a dancing God? How do we join the celebration? Do we dare to believe that Infinite Love is already on tiptoe with expectancy, and that his gaze of love desires to woo us deeper and deeper into intimate relationship with him?

Jesus tells three parables, only recorded in Luke's Gospel, about losing and finding, each one following the other in quick succession. All three tell of the celebrations that follow finding or recovery. It is as if St Luke wants to emphasise certain key elements so that those listening will really get the message. The stories of the lost sheep and the lost coin focus on the diligent search for what has gone missing. The story of the lost son focuses on the father's gaze of love for both sons as he waits passionately for their 'return'. It seems that the only way to express such gladness is to party, and even that doesn't seem to be enough to express the overwhelming sense of joy at the homecoming or bringing back of that which was lost. In the first two parables, friends and neighbours are called in to share in the rejoicing and, in the unseen world, the angels are dancing. But it is the story of the prodigal son that really challenges us to reconsider the nature of celebration and what constitutes real participation.

Both sons are cherished members of the family. One, probably pampered more because he is the younger, is not sensitive to the gaze of love and instantly demands his share of his father's estate. He is not aware of the wound he inflicts on the father's loving heart. The older brother is equally blinded by duty, not so much because of what he feels he has to do, but because he resents the younger sibling shirking his responsibilities while he has to fulfil the expectations placed upon him as the eldest child. So the younger departs, unaware of the devastation he leaves behind, conscious only of the good time he intends to have with his newly acquired wealth. His understanding of celebration is wild living, aided and abetted by his fair-weather friends. There is no heart to it, however, as he discovers when famine hits and all his money is gone. He, who had seized immediate gratification, without a thought as to the consequences for his own life or the lives of those who love him, soon discovers that, having wasted his inheritance, his house has been built on sand. There are no real foundations in his life any more, nothing to draw upon. He finds himself, both literally and metaphorically, in the pits. What he thought would have given him life has resulted in death for him. He has never before faced up to his shadow side. He probably does not even know that he has one.

In the pigsty, with all his grand ideas trampled in the muck, he has time to reflect. One day, devoid of hope, totally alone and destitute, he has a flash of recognition. The word 'recognise' means to know again. He remembers. Something in him that had been inactive, disused and forgotten is revived. He becomes aware of the real treasure he has squandered – the love and acceptance of his father. This is his tipping point. He slowly awakens to the gaze of love. It had always been on him, but he has blinded himself with superficial highs and with the disorientation, nightmares and self-pity that accompany his 'detox'. He repents, that is, he sees thing differently. He now knows, in a place beyond his mind, what really matters.

Clothed in humility and vulnerability, he makes the decision to return to his father's house. He is still a long way off when something incredible happens. The father has never given up watching for his beloved son's return. One day, his passionate vigilance is rewarded. From a distance, the loving gaze recognises the unmistakable figure, albeit no longer well clad or with the confident swagger with which he left. There is no lovelier picture of the love of God in the Bible than that of the father running to embrace the one who 'once was lost but now was found, who had been blind but now could see'. The compassion, the mercy, the love of the father rushes to welcome him, not as a slave but as the beloved. The son's well-prepared confession and plea for some sort of restoration is cut off midway by the father's delight at his homecoming. He is given robe, sandals and ring, signs of family membership and honour. A great feast is prepared (the calf is slaughtered!), the music strikes up and the dancing begins. Restored to life, awakened to the fact of his own belovedness, to his place in the father's house, he is commissioned to pick up the duties, responsibilities and joys of sonship once more. In other words, he has experienced resurrection.

The younger son had gone away full of his own importance, pride and selfishness. Life had been easy at home and, to him, the future looked golden. The distant country so enticed him that he set out for it without a backward glance at the real treasures he was leaving behind. When famine hit and both friends and funds were gone, he experienced brokenness on a scale that is hard to imagine. It was a broken, sadder, wiser man who made his way back home, wondering how he would be received. When all his preconceived ideas of how he might be treated upon reaching the father's house were turned upside down, he was set free within himself to truly celebrate. Great love (stemming from the father's gaze) and great suffering (his own) meet. Something is released within his spirit. The poet Hafiz says, 'No one can resist a Divine invitation. That narrows down all our choices to just two. We can come to God dressed for dancing or be carried on a stretcher to God's ward.'[1] The younger son has been dressed for dancing by the forgiveness, the loving welcome and the generosity of the father. He knows himself both broken and beloved. He is still hurting, not at what happened while he was away, for what he had brought upon himself, but with the ache of knowing, in his recently explored depths, how his attitudes and actions had wounded the ones he loved the most. Pain and joy are partners within him as he takes to the dance floor where there is enough room for all. He dances the pain and the joy with everything that is in him. His brokenness is recognised as gift – he has learned how to celebrate.

Perhaps there is no other way. Most of us will have experienced a form of self-exile in one way or another, either through our own deliberate action, or through the attitudes and actions of others. If we are on the road to becoming fully human and fully alive I doubt it is possible to escape at least one such devastation. At first it can seem like a death, with all hope gone. It is all the more heartbreaking when we reflect, recognise our shadow side and realise that we are in exile largely because of our own actions and the choices we have made. At some point, as we face the reality of how and where we are, a pinprick of light can emerge in a memory of 'home'. Slowly we begin the journey back, sustained, although we are scarcely aware of it,. by the gaze of love. It is only in retrospect that we realise we have never passed beyond the boundaries where God's love can reach and bless us. Even in the distance we have created, we are still held within the gaze. It is also only in retrospective thanksgiving that we recognise the treasures of darkness, the riches stored in secret places that we could have discovered no other way. Our well-rehearsed confessions that we hope will regain us entrance into communion are swept away in exuberant welcome. The overwhelming generosity that greets us as beloved daughters and sons restores us to a place of honour.

Leaving home has something to do with our becoming, our 'coming to be', what we think will make us independent and self-sufficient. Our homecoming has something to do with belonging, 'longing to be' at home in the Father's house, where we discover who we really are. At first glance it may seem as if we face an insurmountable obstacle. If two of the major forces in our psyche are the desire to belong and the desire to become, they appear to be in tension. It might seem as if our inner beings will always be in turmoil as we are pulled first one way and then another at any given time. Surely dancing is impossible. Everyone knows that, in dancing, one partner always has to take the lead. How is celebration possible? The secret lies in awakening to the truth that belonging and becoming can actually be dancing partners when the motivating force is love. David Benner writes, in *The Challenge of Becoming Fully Human*, 'Life is lived on the dance floor in the space between longing and belonging.'[2] The dance is the place of intimacy and abandonment. We approach the dance floor with a newfound confidence, paradoxically born out of knowing ourselves broken and beloved, a confidence characterised by awe and humility. Like the younger son, we have learned the heartbeat of celebration.

The older son has never left the father's house, but has never really felt at home there. He has striven to be perfect, obeying all the outer observances of sonship. He has worked hard, is performance-driven and a people pleaser. Although he is equally loved, he does not know it. He has probably resented his younger brother from the time of his birth. He has seen what he interprets as favouritism and is jealous. Although angry at the manner of his brother's departure, he is perhaps relieved that he has gone. Now there will be no more comparisons or competition. He lives as if the younger has never existed, though he cannot avoid sensing the deep sorrow, the patient waiting and the hope of his father for the return of the prodigal. On this particular day, the older son goes as usual to work in the fields. He does not see the weary figure approaching in the distance. Much later, the day's work over, he returns home. As he nears the house he hears the sound of celebration – music and dancing. What's going on? One of the servants informs him of what has happened. The deep-seated anger that has been his companion for so long erupts. He refuses to join the celebrations. He remains outside. The father's gaze of love embraces the revellers and sees that his older son is missing. He goes outside to where he is and begs him to come in, but the son's anger is undiminished. He accuses his father of not appreciating how obedient he has been, how hard he has worked and how he has never been given the opportunity to celebrate with his friends. And then comes the most unkind comment of all, when he blurts out, 'Yet when this son of yours comes back after squandering your money on prostitutes, you celebrate by killing the finest calf we have!' As well as venting his anger, he is letting his father know that he no longer acknowledges that he has a brother.

The older son is invited in, pleaded with even. Outside are the shadows of self-righteousness, anger, resentment, bitterness, stubbornness, jealousy and pride. They hold him prisoner, denying him entrance. He refuses the invitation. He cannot celebrate.

The older son is not dressed for dancing. He still belongs, is still a beloved son, but perhaps he will be one of those who is carried on a stretcher to God's ward. Touch, tenderness, gentleness, compassion and love are all part of the language of intimacy. Mostly they are manifest without words. They are part of the father's nature. Those who allow the gaze of love to nurture these qualities within them become receptive to this silent language, which those who remain locked in their heads have no understanding of. The older son who had lived his whole life under the influence of such expression was a stranger to them. Perhaps he had so much unexplored negativity inside him that he did not want to take down the protective walls he had built up as his way of coping? He is not the only one. Why do we find the language of intimacy so difficult? Maybe for the same reasons. The last words of this parable vibrate with love and suffering when the father says, 'Look, dear son, you and I are very close, and everything I have is yours. We had to celebrate this happy day. For your brother was dead and has come back to life! He was lost, but now he is found!' The only way we can celebrate who we are is through relationship, though revealing to one another our uniqueness, our beauty. The father knows this. In pleading with the older son, he continues to refer to the younger as 'your brother', refusing to give in to the other's smaller self with its sense of rejection and injured pride. He holds out the promise of restoration of relationship that can only be found by coming inside.

After years of believing that I knew the parable of the prodigal son inside out, I find myself, as with so many other parts of the Bible, brought to a halt in wonder. For me, it is an exploration of what celebration is all about. It is vital for community life. In fact, the ability to truly celebrate is at the heart of any beloved community. When the younger son returned, practically the whole household joined in the feasting and dancing. Celebration takes more than one person. It can be a very lonely, even painful place to be if you have something to rejoice about but no one with whom to share your joy.

When I was studying theology in Edinburgh and the final results came out, five of us who had worked closely together in our last year, specialising in Ecclesiastical History, all achieved first-class honours. It should have been a time of great celebration, but the other four were married and had, naturally, other commitments. I can still recall the sense of loneliness and the ache of not having someone to share in the good news. That experience has made me very aware and, hopefully, sensitive to other people's accomplishments or successes. To freely and unselfishly celebrate with another over their good fortune requires a huge generosity of spirit. We find it easier to commiserate with someone in loss, in grief, or in failure than we do to 'throw a feast' in honour of them and what they have achieved, or simply because of who they are. It might be partly because, in such a situation, even unconsciously, we can feel good about helping them. We don't have to show our own neediness and can even feel somewhat superior. It could also be that it requires a generous heart to rejoice fully in another's success or good fortune. Perhaps not many of us are capable of sustaining such an attitude for too long. I am sure the older brother might have been easier to deal with had the younger been treated with less of a welcome, had he been subjected to some punishment, and been made to agree to certain conditions before he entered the father's house. He might have grudgingly agreed to his brother being taken on as a hired servant. That would have given him the opportunity, if he felt like it, to be condescendingly kind at times; it would have kept him locked in his self-righteous prison. For the culprit to be honoured in every way was too much to bear.

To truly celebrate requires an ability to let go, to be open and a little vulnerable. To risk that means the possibility of being wounded, embarrassed, even shamed. Better to be self-contained, to pretend that all is well and not let anyone see the resentment, the sadness, the envy and the longing struggling to come to the surface. Rarely at a celebration is everybody in total harmony. If, like the older son, we have not dealt with some of our own inner demons then they can spill out and affect those around us. To simply be ourselves and to know that, whatever we are feeling, we are accepted and loved can be a great defuser of tension in any gathering. The father's gaze of love sought to convey that message to his older son, but the tension and negativity within him were too great. He could not receive the gaze. The same gaze of love embraced the younger child. He came back, totally open and vulnerable, hiding nothing, knowing that he did not deserve a welcome. I am sure he began to weep as the unchanging love of the father revealed to him, in his state of utter destitution, that he was beautiful. The slow welling up of joy from beneath layers of pain released him to celebrate a homecoming such as he never could have imagined.

It seems to me that there is an essential message here, one that has been mentioned before in this book. It is often those who have known loss and experienced suffering that can embrace joy more readily than those who, like the elder brother, have never walked such a road. That is, apart, perhaps, from very young children who have not yet encountered the inevitable wounds of life, and can therefore abandon themselves to the present moment in sheer delight.

Celebration, regardless of what has happened in the past or what might happen in the future, is the full appreciation of the present moment with all its life, joy and thanksgiving. Like the older son, many of us are so trapped by baggage from the past or so anxious about shadows looming from an ominous future, that we are prevented from abandoning ourselves to the now – just letting go and having the freedom to be silly or giddy. We are so restricted by how we have allowed our life experiences to condition us that we cannot pick up the rhythm of the dance. Jesus, more than anyone, knew how to live in the present moment. There are so many instances of this in the Bible. He especially enjoyed partying with the marginalised, with those called tax collectors and sinners, with the poor, the lame, the blind. He loved attending feasts where the honoured guests were those whom others would deride or ignore. Another occasion of celebration I particularly love is when he sends out seventy-two disciples to spread the Good News. They return, bubbling over with excitement. Jesus exults, his whole being full of celebration, 'O Father, Lord of heaven and earth, thank you for hiding the truth from those who think themselves so wise and clever and for revealing it to the childlike. Yes, Father, it pleased you to do it this way.'

We can gain a good indication of how self-aware, how free in their spirits, how generous and how secure people are in their identity as the beloved, by observing how they celebrate. It is a good marker of the spiritual and emotional health of any group or community. Every time we let go of some of the inherited or self-created baggage, like the younger son did, we experience greater freedom to join the dance of those who are fully human and fully alive. We draw nearer to the heartbeat of 'home'. We pick up the rhythm of our dancing God and enter more deeply into the welcome that has been there the whole time, but that we could not see because of our lack of awareness. It is the gaze of love that welcomes us and that, in the words of the father in this story, changes 'death to life' and 'lost to found'.

NOTE

1. Hafiz, *I Heard God Laughing: Poems of Hope and Joy*, translated by Daniel Ladinsky (London: Penguin Books, 2006).

CHAPTER THIRTEEN

❦

JUST ONE LOOK
(Luke 19:1-10)

In Restoration Ministries, the organisation for which I work, we seek to provide a safe place where people can come and tell their story and know that they have really been heard. They are invited to retreat from those places of defence, where they have sought to hide their brokenness or anguish from the rest of the world. They can simply be themselves, however messy or unacceptable they may deem that to be. In order to risk that, they need to trust, even a little, the welcome that has been given and to know that what is shared is sacred and, therefore, totally confidential.

One of the things I find very difficult in speaking about our ministry is that most audiences want examples, stories of healing and transformation. This is a natural enough desire, but what goes on in the secret place between a person's encounter with their naked self and their opening up to the gaze of love is private. It is their prerogative as to whether or not they share their story. My preference is that the world would 'see' through the fruits of transformed lives, and then be challenged to undertake such a journey themselves. Suffice to say, we only use the stories we have been given explicit permission to share. It is a real joy, for example, in a post-conflict situation like Northern Ireland, to witness those who, having endured unspeakable anguish, are courageously moved from victimhood, through survival to really living. There are others who, for various reasons, self- or other-inflicted, have found themselves at the bottom, lost, isolated, rejected and hopeless, who see no point in living any more. It is holy ground to witness them, under the transforming power of the gaze of love, not only being restored, straightening up inside themselves in the knowledge of who they really are, precious daughters and sons of God, broken and beloved, but also going on to be agents of hope and real change, image-bearers of love and healing, in the wider world. Having themselves experienced the gaze of love, they can then transmit something of that to others.

Something like this happened to a man called Zacchaeus, whose home was in Jericho. His story is found in Luke's Gospel and is so familiar to us that we might feel we know all there is to know about him. According to one of the early Church Fathers, Clement of Alexandria, Zacchaeus was surnamed Matthias by the other apostles and took the place of Judas Iscariot after the ascension of Jesus. That would make sense to me, for surely anyone who had been so touched and influenced to his innermost depths by Jesus, as Zacchaeus was, would undoubtedly have become a follower with a significant future. Also, in the tradition of the Eastern Orthodox Church and some Greek Catholic Churches in the Slavonic tradition, the last Sunday before what they call Great Lent is known as Zacchaeus Sunday. On this Sunday the Gospel that is read is always Luke 19:1-10. The story of Zacchaeus is chosen for two reasons: first, Jesus' call to Zacchaeus to come down from the tree symbolises God's invitation to walk the path of humility, and second, because of Zacchaeus' subsequent repentance. The other fascinating thing is that the name Zacchaeus means pure – the pure and righteous one! His story is therefore used to illustrate the beatitude 'Blessed are the pure in heart for they shall see

God.' That is exactly what happened. In fact, Zacchaeus' story is really that of the reclamation of his name, his life prior to this having been the antithesis of purity, righteousness or right relationships.

So what was it that changed the course of Zacchaeus' life for good? What led up to it? Did something put him into that place of awareness, becoming his tipping over point into a whole new relationship, a whole new journey? Zacchaeus was a very wealthy tax collector. As such, he worked for the occupying forces – the Romans. As well as collecting for their foreign masters, such officials would have often lined their own pockets, charging more than the required levy, robbing an already impoverished people. Their fellow countrymen classed them along with traitors and informers. A natural consequence of this would have been isolation and marginalisation. Certainly Zacchaeus was not a popular figure in Jericho. Despised and hated by his own people, and treated, perhaps, with no more than contempt by his employers, his would have been a very lonely life, caught as he was, by his own volition, between two worlds and accepted in neither. All his wealth could not buy him friendship, respect, peace of mind or happiness. Perhaps his small physical stature also became the butt of others' jokes. No doubt there were times when he wondered if there was something more to life, but how to find that elusive something? And what would he have to give up or go through in order to reach such an unknown and questionable state?

Then, one day, there was a buzz on the busy streets of Jericho. Word spread that Jesus of Nazareth, the itinerant preacher who had been making quite a name for himself, would be passing through on his way to Jerusalem. Zacchaeus would have heard of Jesus because of his position. Perhaps something inside him snapped; all at once it was the most important thing in the world for him to see this man. How could he do it? He would not be able to see over the heads of the crowd and they certainly would not let him through. It was at this point that desire overcame caution. He just had to see Jesus. It was as if his life depended on it – and it did! Ignoring the taunts and ridicule of the crowd, the little man began to run, his desire driving him. In his desperation, gaining ground ahead of the crowd, his eyes lit on one of the many sycamore trees that lined the roadway. Up he climbed, trusting that now he could see and not be seen. There he waited. After some time Jesus and his companions came along the road, surrounded by the curious and eager crowds, all noise and bustle. From the tree, peering through the leaves, Zacchaeus watched as the procession approached. Then something incredible happened. The procession stopped right under his hiding place, and for a moment there was a curious silence, as if everything on heaven and earth was holding its breath. Then Jesus looked up, directly into the overhanging leafy branches, and addressed Zacchaeus by name: 'Come down quickly, Zacchaeus, for I must be a guest in your house today.' The gaze of love had found him. All it took was just one look! This was threshold crossing for Zacchaeus, the transforming moment. Everything else had been leading up to this, and, for him, life would never be the same.

Perhaps you have felt at some point that there must be more to life than what you are currently experiencing but are at a loss as to how to change either your circumstances or yourself. It seems as if things will always remain the same, and you are caught in a sort of resigned despair. It might take some inner crisis or external event of some magnitude for you to pause between the particular stimulus and your response.

You make the decision in this holy moment to open yourself up to a different kind of presence. From somewhere within, you know this moment is an eternity one and is not to be missed. Things that would normally hold you back and make you cautious are abandoned. You risk the misunderstanding, maybe even the ridicule, and climb your equivalent of the sycamore tree; at this point the most important thing in the world for you is to see more – more of Jesus. Perhaps all of heaven and earth are holding their breath in that holy pause, as the gaze of love searches out your hiding place and urges you to come down. The secret is in letting go – letting go of some of your prohibitive attitudes or apprehensions, of the fears, anxieties and grudges that you have clutched so tightly to yourself.

We often make the statement of faith that God honours the desire of the heart. If we cannot recognise such yearning then maybe we need to ask for it. We are not the only ones with the desire, however. When Jesus passed through Jericho that day it was as if his sole purpose for being there was so that he might encounter Zacchaeus. His heart was yearning for Zacchaeus as much or more than Zacchaeus' was yearning for him. There was an urgency about Jesus. It was the urgency of love, a love that in that moment focused his gaze on the tax collector whose moment had come! Could we dare to believe that God's heart is also burning with love for us, that his desire for deeper relationship with us is so great that he comes to where we are, stops and waits and calls us by name? Could we be courageous enough to open ourselves up to the possibility of such intimacy?

Sometimes I think that we in the institutional Church are somewhat like Zacchaeus. We have, to a certain degree, marginalised ourselves. We are either ridiculed or despised, or regarded as irrelevant by the majority of the population. We want to see Jesus, but maybe because of the battering and the brokenness of the years that has been both self- and other-inflicted, we don't want to be seen by those who would dismiss us. Our growth has been stunted and we are, to a certain degree, hiding from the world. Yet underneath all of that we must be lacking something more. Perhaps we need to allow our desire to be recognised and voiced, driving us to let go of the things that keep us in our box, a yearning that causes us to run to the place of encounter where our desire and that of Jesus meet and we can hear our name which is beloved. Is it beyond the bounds of possibility for us to acknowledge the fact that God wants so much to be a guest in our house that he invites himself? One would think that the Church should be the most obvious place to encounter him. Perhaps it is, but we have not been really aware of his presence. We have going through the motions while not fully believing it. Can you begin to imagine what it will be like when God's desire for us and our desire for him meet head on? When Jesus came by, he looked up at Zacchaeus and called him by name. 'Zacchaeus!' he said. 'Quick, come down! For I must be a guest in your home today.' Zacchaeus quickly climbed down and took Jesus to his house in great excitement and joy.

The word that comes to mind when I read these verses is intimacy. I am struck by the intimacy of Jesus' encounter with this man, his calling him by name and his definite inviting of himself to Zacchaeus' home. There is also the intimacy of what is not recorded – the intimacy of silence. We are not told what happened within the privacy of Zacchaeus' house. It is holy ground that is shrouded in mystery. What is certain is that the encounter, the hidden inner work that went on beyond the public gaze, led to huge transformation. In order for such transformation to take place Zacchaeus had, first of all, to climb down. For years he had sought his identity and security in things that had alienated him not only from others, but from his true self. He was competent in his work. He was very wealthy and 'successful'. Underneath, however, nothing could assuage the loneliness, the emptiness, the fear and the shame. Zacchaeus had an address, but he had never experienced what it meant to be fully 'at home'. He didn't have a true sense of identity. He did not know what it was to be confronted and embraced by love. There is a sense in which he was an orphan, carrying with him all the negativity that such a label can bring. On this day, however, he climbed down. He welcomed Jesus not only into his house, but into the innermost depths of his being.

There are many people who have no true sense of identity. They may superficially belong to a family, tribal group or nation. In reality, however, they are like orphans. What they experience in life is alienation, fear of the unknown, the shame of non-being. If these feelings are not addressed, the internal 'monsters' are turned outwards in aggression, violence and anger. The 'orphan syndrome' remains. This syndrome is easily identifiable in Northern Ireland, among many other places in the world. It is rampant in most 'developed' countries whose leadership think they are so advanced and enlightened but, in reality, have lost that deep sense of respect and dignity that still exists in some communities and cultures in what we refer to as the developing world. Can we recognise these feelings in ourselves at times? We may not express them in the same way but they are real nonetheless. Many people end up blaming themselves, leading to a crippling self-condemnation, even self-hatred. These are the actions of those of us who would already describe ourselves as people of faith. Underneath, where no one else can see, there hides something of an orphan in all of us. Like Zacchaeus, we too can have an address but never truly feel at home in that place of intimacy.

Hope tells us there is a way out of such a prison. The secret lies in being willing to climb down, to go on that inner journey, to realise that, in the secret place where the fears and anxieties lurk, there is also a hidden place of intimacy where there can be a meeting of lover and beloved. All it may take is one look. This is a form of prayer, where we embark upon what some have called the prayer of the heart, or contemplative prayer. It is a prayer of descent where we rest in God. This is what Zacchaeus experienced when he climbed down and went to the secret place with Jesus.

One form of contemplative prayer that can lead us to such a place of intimacy is becoming increasingly talked about and practised in today's world, though it is as old as faith itself. It is known as centring prayer. I have a feeling that just as the charismatic or renewal movement was a work of the Spirit for the end of the twentieth century, enriching and gifting us in so many ways, so this centring prayer encounter or divine meeting holds the key to today's living. One practice of prayer does not cancel another out, rather they all form part of the riches that are freely at our disposal. I had read about centring prayer for years, but within the mysterious purposes of God, my attention was drawn to it again just a few years ago. I read a lot more, listened to CDs from those regarded as gurus in the field, and finally knew that I could no longer avoid doing it. So for the last number of years, I have, however stumblingly, sought to come down into that secret place. It is a novel experience to realise that nothing depends on me. All that is required of me is that I turn up, like Zacchaeus, that I let go, and simply make this inner house a place of welcome. The rest is God's responsibility.

Many of us find it hard to let go, to declutter, to come down from the busyness, the plans, the preparations, the concerns about others, the thousand things that crowd into every day, leaving no space to simply abide. It takes a while to get used to the idea that we don't have to be responsible for the outcome, or even to set goals as to what the outcome should be. We do not turn up for rewards or for a spiritual experience or to get inspiration for the next talk. This prayer is simply about our consent. It is not about success or failure. It is more about letting go, about surrender, about abiding, about an act of love, about an encounter with the Beloved beyond our minds that seek always to control everything. Such prayer takes place in depths where we may not even be consciously aware of how and where the Holy Spirit is working.

Zacchaeus may have had promptings over the years to change his lifestyle a little here and there, but it was impossible for him to do so on his own. His way of life had become so ingrained, and, though he dwelt in the house of fear and loneliness, at least it was familiar. Even if he did decide to mend his ways a little, no one would believe him; their reactions to him would soon weaken his resolve. However, when his desire came to the fore, when he let go of the things that held him back, when he yielded to the gaze of love and consented to climb down and welcome Jesus' presence and action within, the result was transformation. It is said that the fruits of centring prayer show themselves in how you act and react outside of your prayer time. In other words, they are experienced in our ordinary everyday life and not during the prayer period. The inner work takes place in the secret place. It cannot do so in the crowded, busy streets of our hectic daily round, but as we practise coming down and welcoming Jesus into the private home within, gradually we will become aware of the importance and the value of such encounter. This may be happening on an unconscious level, but others will gradually notice. In Zacchaeus' case the fruits were immediately apparent. What had gone on between Jesus and himself produced an almost immediate transformation that was evident for all to see. This man, who used to be taunted and marginalised for his stature, his avaricious behaviour and the betrayal of his own people, stood up in front of them all, fearless, with a newfound humility born out of the intimacy that was the treasure within him. He said, 'I give half of my wealth to the poor and, if I have cheated people on their taxes I will pay them back fourfold!' Total transformation! You will always know the friends of Jesus by their fruits.

There is, however, a little caveat. When we make a move to act differently, we must be prepared to be misunderstood. People, by and large, feel they know us. They have us summed up and nicely boxed, leaving no room in their perception for a change in us. So there may be resentment, grumbling or suspicion, as was the case with Zacchaeus. Because the good citizens of Jericho had summed up and dismissed Zacchaeus as a thief and informer, leaving him no room for change, they questioned Jesus' discernment. 'He has gone to be the guest of a notorious sinner! You would think, if he is a prophet, he would know!' Well, he did know. His gaze of love had sought Zacchaeus out before he changed. It was the same gaze of love that empowered the transformation in him. Jesus saw Zacchaeus as he was and as the person God had created him to be. He knew the hidden depths and possibilities. He did not listen to the complaints but went like an arrow to its target and the resulting fruits were plain for all to see. And Zacchaeus saw him. There was a mutual seeing, out of which flowed the declaration of a truth that Jesus had known all along: 'This man also belongs to the family of God. To him today, to his house, has come salvation; that is, in his letting go, his climbing down, his encounter [which will be ongoing] has come a whole new awareness of who he is, part of a common humanity, broken and beloved.' The transformed Zacchaeus had no need to clutch on to the various defence mechanisms that had been the source of his security and false identity for so long. His unlearning had begun. Out of recognising the fact that he belonged and that he was beloved, the shame of non-being was replaced by a newfound humility, which enabled him to stand with compassion and awareness in front of the crowd and pledge himself to walk the path of mercy, justice, truth and peace. Zacchaeus – the pure and righteous one, his true name reclaimed – was blessed.

Sometimes I wonder if some of the valuable work that many have been doing on this island of Ireland in the field of reconciliation could be seen partly as a patch-up job. This is not to discredit the heroic efforts or the years of working at building relationships and deepening understanding. Can you even begin to imagine where we might now find ourselves without these courageous, humble, hope-filled peacemakers? There has been much change – thank God – but has there been transformation? It seems sometimes as if all our efforts have not gone deep enough to get to the roots of the sectarianism, which is fed by fear of the unknown and a negative sense of identity. The smouldering discontent that rapidly surfaces at the slightest provocation is the outer manifestation of something much deeper.

However, in comparison with other anguished and traumatised areas of the world, we have been given so much.

How many times over the last forty-eight years has Jesus stopped under the tree that is Northern Ireland and, in various ways, issued the invitation to come down – down to the place of forgiveness, of reconciliation, of mercy, justice, truth and peace? And how many times has our listening been selective, hearing only what we want to hear and demanding change or transformation from the other but not from us? As part of the Church I can authentically ask: 'Where is the courageous, faith-filled, prophetic leadership that might give others a voice and hope for the future?' The old enemies of caution and fear of being singled out as different don't seem to have gone away, but have seductively lured us back to the silence of saying nothing. We appear to be trapped again in the house of fear, at a loss as to what to do or how to be. Perhaps the Church as a whole needs to pray for an awareness that will lead to the same desire that consumed Zacchaeus, a desire that will not let us rest until we see Jesus afresh. This time we will not see the Jesus that fits neatly into our denominational way of thinking and being, but the Jesus we don't yet know. This is the Jesus who will, if we are in the right space, stop once again in his mercy and his love, under our tree where we may yet hear him say:

> Church of God make haste and come down, down to that place of repentance and renewal, down to that place beyond all your heady arguments, your rules and regulations and your vain striving after a heartless purity, down to where I am longing to reclaim you as my Beloved, down to where you consent to my presence and action within, to that sacrament of encounter that will lead to transformation.

This is the way of humility, openness and vulnerability, the way of letting go. It is the way that Jesus walks. When we can welcome him without conditions into the house of the Church, into new depths that begin the process of transformation – not on our terms but his – then we will have a different lifestyle, one that is attractive, open, inclusive, joyful and generous, one that will give hope and a whole new awareness to a community that has 'forgotten', often through our negligence, who he is. It may also put us in the place of danger or rejection or misunderstanding from those in church or state who want to cling to their power, or from those who refuse to relinquish the intimidation that keeps people and places under their rule and supplies them with a livelihood.

How do we move towards the beloved community within our own inner beings, within the Church, within the six counties of Northern Ireland and within the island of Ireland as a whole? Is it pie in the sky to dare to believe that a mutual friendship and love is possible in the fragmentation that is me, that is the Church, that is Ireland? Is it too late to hope for a generosity of spirit, a bent towards mercy, a mutual letting go of ancient wrongs, real or imagined, for the sake of this God-given moment? It is all that we have and yet it is enough if we truly believe in this God-man who walks through our world longing for intimacy, who stops under the tree of our individual and collective life with his challenging gaze of love, and is willing to go through Passion and death that we might know that transformation is possible. How do we fulfil our destiny as the family of God on this island? All it may take is one look!

ANSWERED BY
THE GAZE OF LOVE

✼

CHAPTER FOURTEEN

A DIALOGUE OF LOVE
(Luke 10:38-42; John 11:17-44)

Briefly in the Gospel of Luke and slightly more often in the Gospel of John, we encounter the formidable woman, Martha of Bethany. We have, perhaps, done her a disservice by portraying her as the epitome of busyness, while her sister Mary is contemplation personified. It suits our homiletic thinking to label and tidily box these two into different, opposing categories, which then act as our preaching tool to urge people to be more like Mary who sat at Jesus' feet. To do so is to relegate them to a category that is less than human, a place that allows neither of them to change or grow, especially Martha. Some mystery always lingers around Mary, but we think we have Martha sussed! This patron saint of housewives is, to most minds, eternally busy, with little time for reflection. In our unthinking portrayal of her, she is not someone we seek to emulate, whereas many of us yearn to be like her sister who seems to have a special place in Jesus' heart and understands him more than most. This summary of these two close followers and friends of Jesus is, to say the least, simplistic.

Martha, Mary and Lazarus were close friends of Jesus. Their home was a haven for him in the midst of his busy life. It was here he was able to relax in the intimacy of friendship, away from the relentless pressures and demands of his public ministry. Theirs was a house of hospitality where the sharing of a meal was a pivotal event. This was central to ancient Middle-

Eastern culture. Needless to say, all the stops were pulled out whenever Jesus visited. It was one of Martha's gifts, her way of showing Jesus how much she respected and loved him. This was how she could best express her feelings. On this occasion, Jesus was on his way to Jerusalem. He stopped with them and Martha was full of bustle preparing a big dinner. Mary, however, was taking full advantage of his visit, sitting at his feet and hanging on his every word. Eventually it all got too much for the harassed sister. She burst in on them. 'Lord, doesn't it seem unfair to you that my sister sits here while I do all the work! Tell her to come and help me.' Jesus replied, 'My dear Martha, you're getting upset over all these details. Only one thing is needful.' Only one thing. Martha's way of responding to Jesus' presence was to prepare the biggest and best dinner she could. From this encounter it seems as if she based her sense of worth on what use she was. Her busyness controlled her. She was its prisoner. She did not have the freedom to join her sister and simply be.

Martha, it appears, had the wrong end of the stick. She thought, just like the rich young ruler, that by doing more she'd discover the secret of life in its fullness, when really it was about doing less. She was a good and dear person, a worthy member of her community and her place of worship, anxious about doing the right thing. It was Mary who had discovered that the key to eternal life, a life that begins right now and not at some vague point after death, lay in letting go of those things that sought to possess and restrict her. She chose to respond to the gaze of love, to be present to the loving Presence, to be nurtured in that sense of communion with the Beloved. In doing so she displayed a childlike trust, free to simply be. I'm sure there were times when Martha envied her. On this occasion it all became too much. She felt ill-used and her frustration and anger mounted, leading to the outburst. It is a natural enough response, especially if we feel we have been doing our best and are not appreciated or understood. Jesus and Mary would be partaking in the dinner later, so why could Mary not have offered to help her so that they would both have had a chance to enjoy his company? One of the many things I gleaned from this encounter is that it's alright to shout at God. He already knows what we are feeling, so we are only putting words on what we already know. We do not need to do lots of elaborate things to please God, like going to more meetings, or trying to fit in all the demands on our time. The call is always to a deeper communion, so that when things become chaotic, as they often do in life, we are able to draw on that inner well of encounter.

Perhaps Martha is somewhat set in her ways regarding how things should be done, but to sum her up after that brief cameo in Luke's Gospel is not to deal fairly with her. When we turn to the Gospel of John, Martha assumes a greater reality and, with that, something of the mystery that makes us human. It is the essence of humankind that there is always more to discover about a person, more to be revealed. Here, Martha emerges as somebody who cannot be defined simply by her role as a perfectionist housekeeper. What is not in question is her frankness, which we saw displayed in the scenario from Luke. With Martha what you see is what you get. However, in John's Gospel there is so much more to her; we begin to see why Jesus, in his humanity as well as his divinity, loved her.

I like to focus my thoughts of Martha more on the occasion of her brother's illness and death than on the occasion when she got annoyed with her sister (although both, as I've said, are part of her humanity). Lazarus has fallen ill and Jesus and his disciples, whom the sisters would naturally and immediately have turned to, are not near Bethany when this happens. In fact, they are on the other side of the Jordan River, near the place where John the Baptist first preached. They receive a message that Lazarus' illness seems very grave, even terminal. Jesus doesn't set out immediately, even although these three are his closest friends. The message says, 'Lord, the one you love is very sick.' Loving the three of them as he does, it seems strange that he waits two more days. He knows what he is about and, even though he knows Lazarus has died, he believes that God will use this tragedy for his glory. 'Lazarus is dead,' he says to the disciples, 'and for your sake I am glad I wasn't there because this will give you another opportunity to believe in me. Come, let's go see him.'

It is four days after Lazarus' death and burial before Jesus and his disciples arrive at Bethany. Bethany was less than three kilometres from Jerusalem. The small family were well known, so many people had come from the city to pay their respects. As Jesus approaches, word of his coming spreads and Martha hears it. She immediately goes out to meet him, while Mary remains in the house. With her usual directness, and out of her great sense of loss, she says the thing that is uppermost in her mind. 'Lord, if you had been here, my brother would not have died.' It's an accusation arising from her deep sorrow and confusion and also, perhaps, hurt that Jesus has not come sooner. We tend to stop with that sentence, but then she says something else that fills the reader with amazement and the feeling that perhaps we have not done this woman justice. She adds, 'But even now I know that God will give you whatever you ask.' What a statement of faith! Though she may not have sat at his feet as often as Mary, Martha begins to emerge as someone who was listening, reflecting and experiencing a dawning awareness as she busied herself about the house. Could we even begin to think of her as, perhaps, an active contemplative?

In spite of all that is going on around him and within him, Jesus is totally present to Martha in this moment. He gently challenges her and stretches her further than she thinks she can go, by saying, 'Your brother will rise again'. At first she hears this statement as a platitude, one we sometimes hear at funerals, and responds in like manner, 'Yes when everyone rises on resurrection day'. This doesn't help with the deep sense of loss and wondering how she will go on living without the presence of the one she has loved so much. She soon realises, however, that Jesus never wastes time on pious platitudes. He continues, looking at her directly with the gaze of love and uttering the words that for us, over two thousand years later, carry with them an outrageous hope and promise: 'I am the resurrection and the life. Those who believe in me, even though they die like everyone else, will live again. They are given eternal life for believing in me and will never perish.' Then he adds a direct question from which she cannot escape: 'Do you believe this, Martha?' He's drawing her out even further. The question is for her growth. He is inviting her deeper into mystery, further into a heart understanding of what believing is all about and what he is all about. Martha responds to the challenge. We can almost see her grow in spiritual stature before our eyes. 'Yes, Lord. I have always believed you are the Messiah, the Son of God, the one who has come into the world from God.'

Before this encounter and dialogue, Martha believed. However, in her present darkness, she can't allow her belief to move to limitless possibility, light and freedom. This is a very natural response. Then a remarkable thing happens. As

Jesus challenges her, she begins to soar. The wings of her faith are caught by the breath of the Spirit, who is the resurrection and the life, and she sees beyond. 'Yes, Lord, I believe.' Like the disciples, Martha is given another 'opportunity' to believe in Jesus, and her response doesn't disappoint. She is given a bird's-eye view of the Kingdom, of the dream in the heart of God. Think what we would have missed in the subsequent centuries if Jesus and Martha had never had this dialogue, or if it had not been recorded for us in this Gospel. At every funeral I have ever done or attended, Jesus' words to Martha are repeated. Somehow they penetrate the sense of grief, loss and deep sorrow with the light of hope. Famous writers and poets have used these words to inspire and move as, for example, in Charles Dickens' *A Tale of Two Cities*. As Sydney Carton falls victim to the terror in the French Revolution, giving his life so that another may go free, these are some of the last words on his lips. Countless unknown 'saints' facing torture and death have, in their last moments, been steadied and upheld by the words: 'I am the resurrection and the life.'

Martha has nothing to hide. She speaks her mind. Jesus is nearing the end of his earthly life. He already knows, even before the raising of Lazarus, that this specific act will lead to his death. It will be the tipping point for the authorities to put their plans for his destruction into action. It must have been a stark but genuine comfort to Jesus to have this woman, whom he loved dearly (albeit in a different way from her sister), declare her belief. Once she has spoken to Jesus, Martha knows that it is now her sister's turn to be with him. She goes to where Mary is surrounded by a crowd of mourners. She calls her aside from the cries, the whispers and the curious and says, 'The Master is here and wants to see you.' Mary immediately goes to him. Martha acts as an apostle here. She is proclaiming the good news to Mary that Jesus is here, and is present for her.

Martha and Mary could be said to represent our entire faith life – the calling to action and contemplation that are the heartbeat of our vocation. We have all known the struggle of trying to attain balance between the two. The intricate weaving of both strands can be especially difficult for those of us who are 'professionals' – members of religious orders, ministers and priests. We feel that we have striven so hard to be faithful, yet right now it can seem that, no matter what we have done, we are either dead or dying. Like Mary and Martha, we may have 'sent messages' to Jesus, prayers of entreaty, 'Lord, the one you love is sick', but these appear to have been met by silence. We have wrestled with our constitutions, our mission statements, sought new ways to be witnesses to the Good News – distorted into bad news by those lacking a heart understanding of the Gospel – all seemingly to no avail.

Not only within the Church of which we are a part, but certainly on the island of Ireland – at one time known worldwide for its faith and fervour – it seems that in relation to God, in terms of living a vibrant faith, we are either anaesthetised or, at very least, asleep. Surely God who called us into being has not abandoned us? He will come and rescue us and all will be well again. When this doesn't happen, the relentless seeping away of the life we once knew and loved is almost too painful to bear. Caught in grief, a sense of loss and confusion, we too could cry out: 'Lord, if you had been here, this wouldn't be happening. Why didn't you come before we reached such a state?' This confusion could be compounded by the unspoken, precious assumption that our Church, order, denomination or community provided a 'safe place' for Jesus to rest, a place of intimate friendship and communication with the Beloved. Was it all our imagination? Have we been deceived? These are very real questions that we are unwilling to acknowledge, but need to as a first step towards replacing our despair and misery with hope.

The other vital step is to hear the message, 'The Master is here and wants to see you.' I wonder if we can really hear it? Instead of brushing it aside with the reactive response, 'What's the point? It's too late now', could we allow it to sink from our heads to our hearts? This happened to me some time ago. I was sitting in an ecumenical service and a Lutheran pastor from Finland was reading this Gospel. She did not highlight these words but they came into my consciousness and lodged themselves in my heart. 'The Master is here and wants to see you, Ruth.' These are awesome, life-giving, hope-creating words if we dare to really listen. What do they mean for you, for me?

They mean that Jesus is totally present right now. He is here and we are resting in the gaze of love – unconditional, limitless, intimate love. If we can allow ourselves to become aware of this fact, even a little, then we will begin to see how everything changes. Bringing with us all that we have lived – both the joy and the pain – right now the Master is here and wants to see us. When he looks at us he sees his beloved. That is who we are, the name given to us by an all-seeing, all-loving God. That word is not just a description, beautiful as that may be. It is also a challenge, a vocation that will endure when every other secondary vocation is cast aside: be loved, beloved. Accepting the fact of our belovedness is the radical core of the Gospel, the reason why Jesus came. Only when we truly accept it for ourselves can we begin to pass it on to others as Good News.

Through all her encounters with Jesus – those recorded and those known only to her and God – Martha began to pick up this vocation to be loved. A short time afterwards, in the final week of Jesus' life, we find him again in Bethany at a dinner prepared in his honour. Lazarus is at table with him, restored to life. Danger is in the air, not only for Jesus but also for Lazarus. The leading priests are also planning to kill him, for they realise he was the cause of many now believing in Jesus. Whenever I read these few verses in John 12, I get the sense that, even though there was so much disturbance and emotion in the air, Martha and Mary had found themselves in a new way. Mary is free to do what her heart dictates. She emerges from the shadows, disregarding the culture of her day and anoints Jesus with costly perfume. In this extravagant act she is declaring him to be the Christ. It is a prophetic act. The fragrance fills the room, more powerful than any words. From Martha there exudes a sense of peace. No doubt she has done most of the preparation for the dinner, but all that we are told is that 'Martha served'. There are no outbursts of frustration or complaints, she simply serves. She has had her moment of recognition of who Jesus is and she knows herself beloved. She is set free to do and to be without compulsion, but simply out of love. She has come home to herself through presence, encounter and dialogue. This relationship is not broken by death and eternal life begins for her right now

We are not called to be like others but rather the true self that God has had in his mind and heart for us from the very beginning. For us, as for Martha, the key lies in presence, encounter and the dialogue of love, which is largely a silent language. As we open ourselves to the Beloved in such a way, we too begin to soar and say 'Yes, Lord, we believe'. We are found, and find ourselves, in a new way.

❈

CHAPTER FIFTEEN

UNLESS I SEE ...
(John 11:16; 14:1-7; 20:24-29)

From the beginning of recorded history, humankind has had difficulty coping with diversity. It is easier for us to categorise individuals and groups, keeping them 'in their places', without leaving any room for exceptions. In so doing we dehumanise them to some degree, dismissing the parts that don't easily fit in with our preconceived ideas. This stems partly from fear – perhaps fear of the prophetic voice that disturbs our peace, or fear of difference, which has been the root of so many hate crimes throughout history. It is also true to say that, almost subconsciously, we shun self-reflection and scapegoat others rather than facing our own shadow. We not only label people who are alive today, we do so with those who have gone before us. One person who was stigmatised and labelled from the very beginning was the apostle Thomas. Down through the ages he has been referred to as 'doubting Thomas', conveying the impression that, somehow, he wasn't quite on a par with the other ten apostles.

The first three Gospels only record Thomas' name among the twelve disciples. It is to the fourth Gospel that we owe what little we know of him. He first emerges as an individual when Jesus and the disciples receive news that Lazarus is very ill. They are quite a distance away from Bethany at the time. After waiting for two days, Jesus says to his disciples, 'Let's go to Judea again', but they all object. They know that the last time he was there the religious leaders were trying to kill him. They are also probably afraid for their own lives. Jesus, referring to what is up ahead for him, talks about the importance of living the life of faith fully while there is time, and he says he is still with them. Then he adds, 'Lazarus is asleep. But I will go now and waken him up.' They think this means Lazarus is recovering, as evidenced by a good night's sleep, so he has to spell it out clearly for them. 'Lazarus is dead. But for your sakes I am glad I wasn't there for this will give you another opportunity to believe in me.' Then he says, 'Come, let's go see him.'

Jesus knows exactly what he is doing and what the consequences will be. This is the point of no return for him. If he calls Lazarus back to life, his fate is sealed. Enter Thomas. His interjection here has often been interpreted as a statement of despair or fatalism. However, I think Thomas is only voicing what all the others are thinking but don't have the courage to say. It is also a statement of loyal and loving allegiance from him. He is committed to following, as he promised, wherever the way might lead. He says to the other eleven, 'Let's go too and die with Jesus.' Even although they went, I am sure that none of them had the faintest idea what that decision would mean, for Jesus primarily, but also for them.

Thomas, and the others at that point, stayed with Jesus, even though to all intents and purposes it seemed a crazy thing to do. Sometimes it can happen to us too – we are faced with a decision about which way to go on our particular journey in life or faith. It may happen many times. Common sense may tell us to take the obvious and safer route, but if we are attentive we can hear an almost discernible whisper, urging us to choose the road less travelled. Such a decision may be dismissed by others as foolish. Something within us knows we must go by this route, even if it is not understood, even if it means rejection, marginalisation or danger. I believe that the grace of God hides from us what the future will hold. In that sense, we can empathise with the disciples who, if they knew what was to come, would have tried to persuade Jesus to remain where he was. If we knew our future, we probably wouldn't take that particular route either. Perhaps Thomas could be described, among other things, as the patron saint of pilgrims.

We next find Thomas with Jesus and those closest to him on the evening before Jesus' arrest. The disciples are together with Jesus in the upper room. Judas goes out into the night to undertake his dark deed. There is a sense of apprehension in the air and emotions are running high. Jesus has blown the disciples' minds this evening by washing their feet, a task usually left to the lowest slave. He has used the action to illustrate what servant–leadership, the sort of leadership he is inviting them to, is like. He then predicts betrayal and denial. The disciples are confused, upset and unsure. Afterwards, as so many times before, Jesus begins to teach them. He is trying to imprint certain things on their minds, to lodge them in their hearts so that they will not forget. We then have what commentators call the 'farewell discourses'. Breaking into their wonderings, fears and questions, Jesus speaks the words that have become so precious to all those facing hard trials, separation or death:

> Don't be troubled. You believe in God, now trust in me. There are many rooms in my Father's home, and I am going to prepare a place for you. If this were not so, I would tell you plainly. When everything is ready, I will come and get you, so that you will always be with me where I am. And you know where I am going and how to get there.

Can you imagine yourself as one of the disciples at that moment? You might be thinking, 'What is he talking about? This is very profound and mysterious and I can't understand it. Where is this house he's talking about? I want to be with him but just now I feel lost and a bit afraid.'

It is Thomas who again interjects – or interrupts! 'No, we don't know Lord. We have no idea where you are going, so how can we know the way?' Perhaps he senses that events are moving at lightning speed, that everything is changing and he needs to understand. He is not afraid to ask and, again, is merely voicing what the others would like to ask but haven't. There's a bluntness about him, an honesty and a courage. I am sure that Thomas' plain speaking and authentic questioning must have warmed the heart of Jesus, who responds with one of the most precious recorded statements we have in the whole of the New Testament, 'I am the way, the truth and the life. No one can come to the Father except through me. If you had known who I am, then you would have known who my Father is. From now on you know him and have seen him.' This is the best known of the 'I am' statements of Jesus. It has been used to comfort, challenge, encourage and reassure countless people throughout the ages. We could spend the rest of our lives pondering it and still not have plumbed its depths. In a sense, it sums up the Good News: who Jesus is; why he came; the fact that faith is all about relationship (a relationship of mutual love and trust); and that Jesus himself is the supreme revelation of God, that in him we see the face of God.

If Thomas had not asked the question, not only the disciples huddled together that night wondering if their world was falling apart would have missed out, but every person ever since who has heard the invitation to follow, to come with

Jesus. The word 'quest' forms part of the word 'question'. Quest implies a searching and a seeking, a determination to keep going until one is able to understand, that is, to stand under the mystery. Quest is not simply about the head – it also involves the heart. Its beginning is in the form of revelation and its ending is renewed revelation. Thomas was on a quest that would last all his days and beyond. He was a seeker and a searcher. We owe him so much. It could be said that one of his chief gifts was asking questions. I remember hearing the story of some students in a theological college. One day, one of them anonymously wrote on the board 'Jesus is the answer'. When they reassembled for class, another, also anonymously, had written below, 'Yeah, but what is the question?' Thomas reminds us that asking questions, wrestling with faith, and not being satisfied with clichés or pat answers is a vital part of the journey. Jesus himself indicates this when he says, 'Ask and you will receive; seek and you will find; knock and the door will be opened.' The relationship to which he invites us is not without struggle. Sometimes it's very hard, but the unfolding friendship is the Way for us, the Truth for us, Life for us. Once more, we see Thomas as the patron saint of the seekers and the searchers.

Ten days have passed and so much has changed. The friends of Jesus have lived through an unspeakable nightmare and have arrived at a place of outrageous hope. The upper room is still their meeting place. Even though they deserted Jesus and were scattered after the public execution of their beloved Master, they gravitate back to that room, as if trying to hold on to some of the memories of the One who had meant the world to them. They gather in secret, all except Judas, and they lock the doors. They are still terrified that they will be identified as companions of Jesus and the same fate could await them. Unable to stay away, yet unable to publicly declare their allegiance, they huddle together, each trying to draw some comfort or strength from the other, all wondering what the future holds.

On the first day of the week after the crucifixion, we find them there, all except Thomas (and, of course, Judas). All of a sudden Jesus is standing there among them! They know it is him and yet it cannot be! He speaks the familiar greeting, 'Peace be with you'. They are in shock, dumbfounded and terrified all at once. To prove that it is really he, Jesus holds out his hands. There is no mistaking those nail marks. He shows them his side where the piercing had taken place. Incredulous joy begins to spring from grief, guilt and fear. 'Peace be with you,' he says again, 'as the Father has sent me, so I send you.' Amazingly, after all that has happened, he still trusts them. He's recommissioning them. He then gifts them with the breath of the Spirit, enabling them to become image-bearers of forgiveness, perhaps the most important message for the world, both then and now. Life can never be the same for this little group of followers.

They haven't all had this marvellous experience, though. Thomas isn't there. Where is he? Perhaps he too is behind locked doors, though of a different sort. He is dealing with the legacy of grief and self-blame. He is the one who said, such a short while ago, 'Let's go with Jesus and die with him', but when it came to the crunch, he ran away. It is no matter that the others did the same, Thomas is wrestling with his own part. He is locked in despair and remorse, without hope and in desolation. We might say he is suffering from post-traumatic stress disorder. He seemingly has gone off on his own, unable to bear the presence of the others who remind him so forcibly of what has been loved and lost. He cuts himself off from his community and hands himself over to the utter shock and misery of his situation. In doing so he misses the moment. Being so totally present, naturally enough, to his smaller self – his devastated ego with its self-blame, self-doubt, and panic – he is not present to meet with Jesus. When he does return he is met with the overwhelming excitement and joy of the ten apostles, the other disciples, and the women and men who have been companions with Jesus throughout the three years of his public ministry: 'We have seen the Lord!' Thomas can't, or won't, believe them. He knows what has happened and he's not going to be taken in by the delusions of apparitions. Seeing is believing, so he thinks. True to form, he states, 'Unless I see and touch, I will not believe.' Eventually they give up trying to convince him.

The days go by. In spite of the resurrection appearances and the gentle wind of the Spirit, the disciples are still gathering in secret behind locked doors. Their liberation appears to be very gradual. It is not only Thomas who needs more convincing, they do too. What did they do in the waiting period? I think the waiting was a gift to them, even though it may not have seemed like it at the time. They needed the 'holy pause' in order to absorb what had already happened. They needed to be quiet and to allow awareness to surface. Though Thomas was the questioner, perhaps he was the most collected, for he appears to have been more in touch with his shadow side and could voice things that the others couldn't. This makes me think of my experience with centring prayer. As mentioned earlier, this is a prayer practice as old as Christianity itself, where we simply turn up and sit in the presence of the Beloved, of Jesus, and quietly consent to his presence and action within. The disciples turned up and waited, and then Jesus turned up again. Eight days later they are all together in the same place, including Thomas. Jesus appears, like a déjà-vu, with the same greeting, one that is not mere words but conveys substance at the same time, 'Peace be with you'. His gaze then rests upon his beloved Thomas. I imagine it was a look of compassionate understanding, as he addresses himself entirely to the seeker. 'Put your finger here and see my hands. Put your hand in the wound in my side. Don't be faithless any longer. Believe!' There are no half measures with Thomas. Once he recognises who it is, his response is immediate and total: 'My Lord and my God!' he declares and confesses. Sometimes we yearn to see, to really know. For us, like Thomas, we feel that seeing would be believing. In his book on John's Gospel, Jean Vanier says, 'O happy fault of Thomas who did not believe, so that our belief may be founded upon his doubts, which called forth this new apparition of Jesus!'[1]

Then Jesus adds something so precious, spoken directly to Thomas but, in reality, spoken for all who would believe afterwards: 'You believe because you have seen me. Blessed are those who haven't seen me and believe anyway.' This is one of the many hidden beatitudes in the Gospels: 'Blessed are those who have not seen but believe.' It is Thomas to whom we owe this blessing. If he had not been so forthright, then we would not have received it. In blessing Thomas, Jesus blesses all of us. We haven't seen him yet we believe. Our belief may be shaky at times, we know we still have a long way to travel, as did Thomas, but we are assured that that's all right. There is something very liberating about that. Far from being the marginalised one, not quite on a par with the others because of his doubts, Thomas probably had the healthiest attitude to the momentous events of those couple of weeks. It is as if he is encouraging us to keep asking the questions and, if we do, the answers will look after themselves. With the passage of time, we have, rather tritely, caricatured Thomas as the doubter, so much so that the phrase 'doubting Thomas' is generally used today in a pejorative sense. Instead of referring to him as Thomas the Doubter I like to think of him as Thomas the Seeker – my brother Thomas, with me as I search and question and struggle, sometimes rather doggedly because I know that there is no other way then the Way; there is no other truth than the Truth; there is no other life than the Life. I haven't 'seen', I haven't 'touched' but, in the mystery of unknowing, I too dare to say, 'My Lord and my God'.

There is just one other fleeting appearance, one other brief encounter between Jesus with Thomas. It takes place by the lakeside, sometime later. The disciples have returned to their old haunts. Were they awaiting further instructions? Were they waiting on God? Who knows? To fill the time, at the instigation of Peter, some of them decide to go fishing. Seven of them push out from shore, including Thomas. They fish all night and catch nothing, until a stranger on the shore tells them to do things differently, resulting in an enormous catch. Tradition tells us that Thomas was also known as Didymus – Thomas the Twin – because he looked so like Jesus. It is the one St John describes as the 'beloved disciple' who recognises the stranger on the shore. Is it stretching the imagination too much to suggest that as he looked at Thomas in the boat and at the stranger on the shore, the flash of recognition came to him and he shouted out, 'It is the Lord!'?

At the beginning of the Gospel of Thomas, subtitled 'The Wisdom of the Twin', we find these words: 'I who write this am Thomas, the Double, the Twin. Yeshua, the Living Master spoke, and his secret sayings I have written down. I assure you, whoever grasps their meaning will not know the taste of death.'[2] It is not my place here to enter, nor could I, a debate as to the authenticity of this Gospel and the question as to whether it represents another strand, lost but loved, which preserves aspects of Jesus that present him as a powerful teacher of Wisdom. However, I like to think that the Seeker, the Double, the Twin continued with his quest. Indeed we know that his journey as a companion of the risen Lord took him to India. In moving deeper into the mystery of who Jesus is, Thomas grew more and more like him. Is that not the calling, the vocation for each of our lives?

NOTES

1. Jean Vanier, *Drawn into the Mystery of Jesus through the Gospel of John* (London: Darton, Longman & Todd, 2004), p. 345.

2. Lynn Bauman, *The Gospel of Thomas* (Ashland, Oregon: White Cloud Press, 2004), p. 5.

CHAPTER SIXTEEN

TRANSFORMED BY THE GAZE OF LOVE

(Acts 9:1-19)

The gaze of love is omnipresent, not restricted by time or space. Awareness of this truth, both in its intimacy and universality, can change the world, as it has done in the past. One of the most dramatic instances of such an awakening came to Paul, first known as Saul, whose amazing story is found in the Acts of the Apostles. A devout Jew, zealous Pharisee and brilliant academic, he hated the new sect, known as followers of the Way, who seemed to be attracting large numbers. In Saul's eyes they were a danger to the 'purity' of Judaism and should be wiped out before they did too much damage, so he began a kind of personal pogrom. Saul first appears on the scene in the immediate aftermath of Stephen's so-called trial. Stephen, a 'good man and just', was obviously a deeply committed follower of Jesus, so much so that at his trial on trumped-up charges of blasphemy, even those accusing him and lusting for his death could see that his face was like that of an angel. His powerful witness to God's dealings with his people throughout the ages – accompanied by their frequent stubbornness and rebellion, and the culmination of the coming of Jesus who is the Messiah – enraged them. The penalty for blasphemy (their accusation against Stephen) was death by stoning. Enter Saul. We are not told if it was he who engineered the trial and subsequent sentence, but we do know that he appears to be the leader of the mob. Even here he is very cunning. He keeps himself blameless by not lifting a stone to hurl at Stephen, but it is clear he encouraged others and approved of what they did. I am reminded of certain individuals in the conflict in Northern Ireland who showed similar cunning, whipping up the frenzy of the mob to protest, destroy and kill, while keeping their own hands clean and leaving their followers to face the consequences. Those stoning Stephen remove their cloaks, presumably to enhance their aim, leaving them at Saul's feet. He was obviously in total agreement with what they were doing. In fact, at the beginning of Acts, Chapter 8, he is described as one of the official witnesses.

Saul is not aware of it, but the death of Stephen, in particular the way he died, begins to have a powerful, as yet unconscious effect upon him. Reading between the lines of scripture (which may or may not be a dangerous thing to do), I sense what happened was as follows. Stephen prays a prayer of forgiveness as his dying gaze rests upon the chief perpetrator. God's response is, 'Very well, Saul, I have heard the prayer of my faithful servant Stephen and because he has asked it, I forgive you, but now you've got to take over where he left off.' This is exactly what happens. In the aftermath of Stephen's death, persecution of the believers intensifies. The war raging within the subconscious of this strict and zealous Pharisee seems to mirror the relentless persecution without. What follows is well known.

Paul's experience on the road has found its way into the English language when we speak about a 'Damascus Road experience'. On the day Stephen dies, a new wave of persecution of the followers of the Way sweeps through Jerusalem, causing many of them to flee. This is one of the many scatterings of Jewish people that we call the diaspora. The blessing from this seeming tragedy is that the Good News of Jesus Christ, crucified and risen, spreads into all the areas where the fugitives find themselves. For a time the focus of persecution is Jerusalem, with Saul and his entourage fanatically moving from house to house in order to root out the believers and throw them into jail. He casts his vote to have many of them put to death. He has others whipped to try to get them to curse Jesus. There appears to be no act of violence he will not stoop to in order to silence or wipe them out. Soon, however, word filters through from other places, most notably Damascus, that these new people of the Way are having an alarming influence on people there. Saul is incensed. He goes to the powers that be, the Sanhedrin, and requests that the high priest issue letters to the synagogues in Damascus, asking for their cooperation in tracking down and arresting all those believed to be followers of the Way. His intent is to bring them back, both women and men, in chains to Jerusalem. His zeal is unstoppable (a zeal that, ironically, in later years is used to promote the very movement he is now seeking to wipe out!).

Armed with the necessary paperwork and accompanied by the police officers of the Sanhedrin, he sets out for Damascus, a distance of about one hundred and forty miles. If on foot, as it seems they are, the journey would take them about a week. You can imagine Saul's impatience to cover the miles as quickly as possible so that no one might escape. Because he adheres to the strictest of the Pharisee sects he cannot associate with his Sanhedrin guards, so there is plenty of time for his resentment to fester. The way leads through Galilee, which probably deepens his anger and steely resolution, for it was in Galilee that Jesus had lived out most of his public ministry. They are on the approach to Damascus, the major part of their journey over, when something strange happens.

Saul later describes it, on several occasions, as a brilliant light from heaven, shining directly upon him. The suddenness and the brightness cause him to fall to the ground. Lying there, dazed and shocked, he hears, unmistakably, a voice. It says, 'Saul! Saul! Why are you persecuting me?' Saul, stunned and shaken, asks the question, 'Who are you, Lord?' Can you imagine the emotions that surge through him when he hears the response, 'I am Jesus, the one you are persecuting.' Nothing could have prepared him for this. To hear the voice is shocking enough, but to have it identified as that of Jesus of Nazareth, whose followers he is on a mission to exterminate, is beyond his comprehension. Perhaps he might have found it easier to understand if the voice had said: 'Why are you persecuting these innocent people whose only "crime" has been to become my followers?' But to be told that he is persecuting Jesus himself blows his mind.

This is his first introduction to that for which he will later become such a strong advocat – the concept of the body of Christ. When one suffers, we all suffer together, and when we cause pain and grief to those he loves, we are causing pain and grief to Jesus himself. This is something that people today, especially those who claim to be friends of Jesus, would do well to reflect upon afresh, when we consider how many godly people in anguished areas of the world are being attacked, tortured and imprisoned in a similar manner. This means that right now, at this moment, all over the world, Jesus is being persecuted. But the voice doesn't stop there. There follow instructions about what should come next: 'Get up, Saul, and go into the city and you will be told what you are to do.' The strong, arrogant leader on a violent mission is reduced to the state of a helpless child. The light has blinded him; he can no longer see. He who is so used to giving orders and having them instantly obeyed is now under orders. The guards accompanying him are also stunned. They too have seen the blinding light and heard a disembodied voice. They do not know what is going on. The only thing they can do is take the once proud, self-righteous Pharisee by the hand and lead him into the city. This was so different from the way he had planned to come – the zealous orthodox, on fire for the purity of his religion, arriving like an avenging angel to wipe out the enemies of the living God.

The encounter on the Damascus Road is only the beginning of a whole series of events. Around the same time as Saul is being led into the city, a man called Ananias, a follower of the Way, is fervently praying. The news has travelled fast that Saul is on a mission to deal with the believers in Damascus. This would have been weighing heavily on Ananias' mind as he prayed and waited before God. What was going to happen to them all? Would they be strong enough in their newfound faith to withstand persecution of what was fast becoming another religious tradition? What would happen to the newly formed Church if all the leaders were taken away? Ananias does not have a clue as to what has already happened on the Damascus Road. As he reflects and earnestly prays, he hears the Lord call him by name. 'Yes, Lord!' he replies. There follows one of the most explicit commissions in the New Testament: 'Ananias, I want you to get up and go right now to Straight Street, to Judas' house. When you get there you are to ask for a man called Saul of Tarsus. He's praying to me at this very minute and I have told him in a vision that a man called Ananias will be coming to visit him and to lay his hands on him so that he will be able to see again.' There is shocked silence as heaven holds its breath, and then comes the protest, 'But, Lord, surely you know all about this man, the terrible things he has done to the followers of the Way in Jerusalem, and how he's been authorised to do the same to us here in Damascus?' But the Lord says, 'Go and do what I say. For this man is my chosen instrument to take my message to Gentiles and to kings as well as to the people of Israel. And I will show him how much he must suffer for me.' This is a tough assignment! What would you or I have done in these circumstances? Argued a little bit more, prevaricated, made a list of excuses? What we read here are three simple words: 'So Ananias went.' What trust, what obedience, what courage and love! But there's more. Ananias doesn't do things by halves. He finds Saul, lays his hands on him and calls him, 'Brother Saul'. In that action, in those two words, they became companions on the journey.

'Brother Saul' – what reconciling and compassionate words to this enemy who believed in the same God but who had terrorised and threatened and destroyed so much of what Ananias held dear. He then prays for the restoration of Saul's sight and for the gift of the Holy Spirit. Luke tells us that instantly something like scales fell from Saul's eyes. He could see, but there was also a greater seeing. Scales had fallen from his heart as well. He is baptised and welcomed into the body of believers. Stamped with the seal of the Holy Spirit, Saul is now 'under new ownership' – his life is totally surrendered to Jesus. On the peripheries of his old world, he finds himself, for a time, also on the peripheries of the new, the believers naturally being suspicious and afraid. It is Barnabas who takes him by the hand, who risks encounter and dialogue, who introduces him and stands with him before the rather fragile community of the leaders of the Way. The door is now open for Saul to pursue a totally different mission. He does fulfil Stephen's 'defence' at his mock trial. Over time he becomes the great missionary to the Gentile world and in himself a living, dynamic prayer for the reconciliation and unity which is ours in Christ. The key elements in his transformation are forgiveness, encounter, reconciliation, inclusion and dialogue. What generosity of spirit the first believers show and what trust in the mysterious purposes of God! Where did they go from there? Read on in Acts and discover how that trust and obedient faith of Ananias was a crucial step towards a worldwide sharing of the Good News. Think what might or might not have happened had Ananias not been praying, not been listening or, out of fear or doubt, refused to go. Paul, once blind to the Way, to the Good News, now sees. He embraces and is embraced by the culture of a new Kingdom, his spiritual sight grows sharper and keener.

This is the only time we read of Ananias in scripture, but it is enough. He fulfilled his destiny as part of God's great plan. His whole life had been leading up to this point, and, when the moment came, he was ready. I am sure that Saul (now Paul) often looked back to that day, that encounter, and his subsequent welcome by the followers of the Way as his inspiration and encouragement when times were tough. From this point, the conviction began to be nurtured within him that Christ himself made peace between those of diverse cultures, races and national identities. Years later he could write with total assurance: 'He has broken down the wall of hostility that used to separate us. His purpose was to make peace – by creating in himself one new person from the two groups. Together as one body, Christ reconciled both groups to God by means of his death, and our hostility towards each other was put to death.'

Brian McLaren, in a recent book, writes of subversive friendship, that which 'crosses the boundaries of otherness, daring to offer and receive hospitality'.[1] Such action/interaction always involves risk, particularly of being regarded as a traitor to the norms of your group. To be partially or totally ostracised for such commitment can be a rather lonely and frightening thing, but as we practise it, it gradually becomes second nature. There comes a point where we know we have crossed the Rubicon and there is no going back. On the one hand, we may have lost what was very dear to us, that which seemed to be part of our identity and comfort zone, but, on the other hand, such letting go, such unlearning eventually leads to a whole new set of relationships. This was the trust and faith of Paul.

McLaren discusses three components in such subversive friendship: companionship, conviviality and conspiracy. How do we live lives that say, 'You are welcome. It is good that you are here'? One of the chief ways is through the consistent practice of hospitality. In his subsequent letters, Paul urges the small communities of believers to model this, as it had been modelled for him from that eventful day and in so many diverse places. McLaren describes conviviality as 'sharing the gifts of life together with appropriate respect and understanding'.[2] Respect really means taking a fresh look at the other, to see again; understanding indicates a standing under all the impressions and judgements we have made about the other and encountering the mystery of their humanity. It's not just coexistence, but rather being open enough and vulnerable enough to let the other in on you. It is the risk of encounter. So conviviality is not just a superficial camaraderie but something much deeper to which we commit ourselves. It involves listening, humility and a generosity of spirit. It is the challenge of encounter, a challenge that was dear to Paul's heart. It won't happen overnight. It takes years of moving forward, and even when what you've committed your life to explodes in your face, you pick yourself up and keep on going because you know, in a place beyond all formal knowing, that this is the way that has chosen you.

There is even more to subversive friendship – what McLaren describes as conspiracy. I love this image of whispering plans and plots – plotting goodness – what he describes as rehearsing and practising for a better world through the give and take of friendship.[3] It conjures up for me the picture of those of us who are aware of this call to friendship, being God's secret agents, working for the emergence of the upside-down Kingdom. These agents are everywhere, more numerous than we know. Paul and his friends were among the first of them. Many of them are underground as they commit themselves to the prayer that 'lets go and lets God'. It is in such conspiratorial times, when we stop striving and simply consent to God's presence and action within, that a seismic shift begins to take place in the unseen world towards inclusion, unity and peace. Other agents are more obvious as, for example, when their whispering forces them to go public and build relationships with those who are different. As people of faith called to friendship, we are challenged not so much to build a bridge over the troubled waters of division, suspicion, enmity and hatred, but to be in ourselves a bridge. When we do so, however falteringly, we are following in the footsteps of St Paul, but much more than that, we are following in the footsteps of his Lord and ours.

Empowered by the Spirit, awakened by the gaze of love, present to self, to the other and to the Love that draws us, the way we journey is through dialogue, through responding to the call to friendship, a friendship that is willing to risk, to let go, to lay itself down for the sake of the beloved community, through practising the sacrament of encounter. It is not the road of power and control, or of big movements or mass demonstrations. It is a little road, a road of vulnerability and openness, a road of letting go. On the way, as we are awake and practising presence, there will be companionship, conviviality and conspiracy and perhaps another 'c'. We travel with confidence – in Latin *confidere*, meaning to have full trust – and with a faith that assumes total reality in the revelation at our journey's end, which is also a beginning. This is when, as Paul was to write later to the Church in Corinth, we shall see everything with perfect clarity and will know everything just as God knows us right now.

From the point of his conversion, Paul lived his life on the peripheries of an empire that had peaked in greatness and was beginning to show signs of fracture. Zealously and fearlessly, he fulfilled his commission to be a bearer of the Good News wherever the Holy Spirit directed him to go. The records tell us that his life ended in Rome. For me, this remarkable story has its source in the gaze of love from God through Stephen, leading to what we readily underestimate ourselves – Stephen's prayer of forgiveness, followed by that amazing encounter. We have not even begun to tap into the power that there is in such a prayer and process. It releases a dynamic for us that gives us the freedom to be fully alive, to see things differently (the real meaning of repentance), to exercise choice, to be seized by an outrageous hope for this fractured world and an unquenchable passion for reconciliation and unity.

Throughout this book, we have journeyed a long way together and encountered people from the pages of scripture that we thought we already knew. I hope that they have become more alive for us in the process, but, more importantly, I hope that we have encountered Jesus and ourselves in a deeper way.

My prayer would be that as we meet him in all the different scenarios that make up our life, our question would always be, 'Who are you, Lord?' because there's always more to discover, to know of this Jesus who calls us and challenges us and commissions us again and again in love.

NOTES

1. Brian McLaren, *Why Did Moses, Jesus, the Buddha, and Mohammed Cross the Road?: Christian Identity in a Multi-Faith World* (London: Hodder & Stoughton, 2012), p. 212.
2. Ibid., p. 214.
3. Ibid.

EPILOGUE

What if infinite love has set its eyes on you for itself alone?

Lord, when all else is stripped away, it is this for which we
yearn.

Awakened by the gaze of love ...
Hagar sees the Living One who sees her – and her hope is
revived.
Abraham leaves what is familiar and dear – and becomes the
great bearer of the Promise.
Jacob wrestles with his past – and, with a new understanding
of his true identity, is reconciled with his brother.

Under the gaze of love ...
Moses is drawn by a holy curiosity – and is commissioned to
lead a people from slavery to freedom.
Ruth chooses the road less travelled – and becomes a vital part
of God's gift of love to the world.
Elijah is called out from the cave of his inner self – and, seeing
things differently, goes back to the place of his vocation.
The Psalmist is overcome by the omnipresence of God – and
responds with the plea to be searched, known and led.
Infinite Love spans the hundreds of years between Old and
New – and takes on our form and likeness in Jesus.

Called by the gaze of love ...
The first disciples respond to the invitation to come and see
– and so begin a lifelong journey of ever-deepening awareness.
The Woman at the Well, the Man at the Pool and Veronica
straighten up in their inner beings – and become what is in
the heart of God for each of them.

Searched out and recognised by the gaze of love ...
The Rich Young Ruler turns away from its intimate intensity –
and leaves in sorrow.
The Lost Son and Zacchaeus are drawn by that same intimacy
and intensity – back to the Father's house, to homecoming and
celebration.

Answered by the gaze of love ...
Martha and Thomas let go of their questions and doubts – and
are gifted with recognition and surrender.
Paul is turned around, transformed – and becomes the great
light-bearer, hope-giver, and living icon of reconciliation.

We are surrounded by so great a crowd of witnesses to the
empowering of the gaze of love. Let us, then, awaken from our
sleep – and let us keep our eyes fixed on Jesus, whose gaze is
first and always resting upon us.

As it was in the beginning, is now and shall be forever.
Amen.

A PRAYER

Lord, we have travelled far, covered much ground with these, your beloved, who emerge from the ancient pages of scripture and accompany us on the way. Now they are our friends, our companions on the journey.

They give us courage because we see that they too know fear — and keep on going.

They give us hope because we know they are part of a common humanity — as we are; they are ordinary people who become extraordinary, flourished by the gaze of love.

They nurture faith in us, because, like us, they doubt, question, despair, take wrong turns — and yet become part of the unfolding story of your love for humankind.

They bless us because, through your grace and mercy, they are part of the shining company of those throughout the ages who have kept faith and hope and love alive.

They bless us because they have dared to see visions and dream dreams — and, with an outrageous hope, have paid the price to see their dreams come true.

They stand, these faithful companions, our sisters and brothers, in the mystery of the present moment, in the unseen world that is nearer than we know, and with one voice they proclaim as challenge, vocation and assurance for this day, for this now, for us, 'Infinite Love has set its eyes on you for itself alone'.

Amen.

ACKNOWLEGEMENTS

I would like to thank the team at Veritas for all their help and availability during the writing of this book, in particular Donna Doherty and Emma O'Donoghue. The Board of Directors of Restoration Ministries has been continually supportive. My friend Jenny Meegan has been an insightful and attentive listener, and my friend and colleague, Rose Ozo, a constant source of encouragement and vision. Finally, I am deeply grateful to Fr Richard Rohr and Jean Vanier for their endorsement of this book and for their prophetic witness to the gaze of love.